FOREWORD TO THE STUDENT

If you think the stories of the pioneers travelling through the lands of the western Indians were exciting, wait until you read about the voyages and travels of the apostle Paul, who was the first Christian missionary. And think how exciting it would be to get a letter from the apostle Paul or Peter or John! These are the kind of things you're going to be reading this year.

The Materials You Will Need

This book is one of your tools, but it's only your guide. It will tell you what to do and read each week, and it will also give you some questions to answer, and show you where to find the answers. And it will be your notebook where you will write your answers.

The book you're going to be studying is the Bible, and it's the most important book in the world because it was written by God. Actually you're only going to be reading the book of Acts in the New Testament and 21 letters, written by Paul, Peter, John, two of Jesus' brothers, James and Judas, and a man named Apollos. And they are going to talk about the kind of problems you and I and everyone else in the world face, and tell us what to do about these problems. They're also going to explain all about God's plan of salvation.

The New Testament was written in Greek, and therefore we must use translations which turn the Greek into English. There are quite a few of these translations, and while they're all a little different, it really doesn't matter that much which one you use. The most common one is called the King James Version (KJ), and it will sound a little strange because it isn't in really modern English, but you can understand it with a little practice. But if you're going to buy a new Bible or New Testament, you'll find one of the modern translations easier to use and understand. Many of our churches are now using the New International Version (NIV), others use the Revised Standard Version (RSV), or Beck's An American Translation (AAT), or the Good News Bible (TEV). And I have my own translation of the book of Acts and the Gospel of Luke called The Good News And How It Spread (Good News), which I think you will find to be the easiest to understand of all. It's an inexpensive paperback, and there are also paperbacks of the NIV and TEV.

You should also have a dictionary to look up words for which you don't know the meaning. And you should get in the habit of using your dictionary every time you find a word you don't understand.

How To Do Your Work

This course has 31 lessons, each of which will take from two to four hours' time to do before you go to class. Each lesson will cover from one to 13 chapters, and will be a week's work; and the title of each lesson will tell you which chapters you're going to read that week. As you read each chapter there will be questions to answer. If the section heading says Acts 10, it means the tenth chapter of Acts. If it says Romans 8:1-5, it means the eighth chapter of Romans, verses 1-5.

When you come to a new section, the best thing is to read through the entire section rapidly to get the whole idea. Then read the questions in order and write your answers right under the question. Answer each question briefly, but completely. Don't just copy the verse! Put it into your own words, or copy just the part that specifically answers the question. In the parentheses after each question the verse number or numbers are given where you will find that answer, so that you won't have to hunt all over. Vs 1 means verse 1, and vss 3-4 mean verses 3 and 4. Sometimes the verses in the parentheses will have two sentences, or two or more clauses, each marked off by a period, semicolon (;) or a colon (:). In such cases the verse number will be followed by a letter (a or b, etc.) telling you in which part of the verse to look for the answer (a means the first clause or sentence, b, the second, etc.). Sometimes you will find a reference to some other book of the Bible, and some will be to Old Testament books. The abbreviations will be obvious, but if you don't know them all, the names of all the books are found in the index in the very front of the Bible. In some editions there will be an index at the beginning of the Old Testament, and another at the beginning of the New Testament. If you use The Good News And How It Spread for Acts, you'll have to use some other version for the letters and Old Testament references.

You must prepare every lesson, however, at home before you go to class. And you should write your answers in pencil, and then take an eraser along to class, so that you can erase any parts which are wrong and put in the correct answers. That's the purpose of the class discussion - to be sure that every student has all the correct answers when the class is over.

One word of advice. Don't put off all your home preparation until the night before it's due! The easy way is to do a little bit each day, or do it in two or three sittings. That way you won't need so much time any one day. And as you work, take time to read each question carefully before you answer the question.

Key Questions

One last thing. All the questions and answers are not of equal value or importance. That's true no matter what you're studying. Therefore when your teacher tells you to circle or mark certain questions in each lesson, these are the "key" questions and answers. That means that you should memorize the answers to these questions, and review them each week to make sure you don't forget them. Learning the key questions is what the course is all about. If your teacher has a review each week, the reviews will cover these key questions. And when you finish the 31 lessons, and begin to fill in the Summary (Lesson 32), you will find all the words for the blanks in these key questions. Also any tests your teacher gives will consist of these key questions. Therefore if you will take time to memorize the answers to these key questions, you will get a good mark on the reviews and tests, and more important, you will have a good understanding of the Book of Acts, the earliest history of the Christian Church, and all the letters written by the apostles, who were repeating what Jesus Himself taught them. And most important of all, you will have a good understanding of God's plan of salvation.

May God the Holy Spirit bless you and help you as you do these lessons each week!

Julian G. Anderson

LESSON 1 - ACTS 1-2

Jesus Gives His Orders and His Spirit to His Church

May-June, 29 A.D.

Chapter 1

1. Read vss 1-5. Who must have written this book? (Compare vs 1 with Luke 1:1 Good News; 1:3 KJ, RSV, NIV, Beck).

2a. What was his first book about? (vs 1a)

   1.

   2.

b. Where did he begin the story? (See Luke 1:5-17)

c. Where did the first book end? (vs 2a)

3a. What had Jesus been doing just before His ascension? (vs 3a)

b. To what great event was He thus pointing them? (vs 3a, see Luke 24:1-8)

c. What had He done to convince them? (vs 3b)

4. What orders had He given His followers on one occasion?

   1. (vs 4a)

   2. (vs 4b)

5a. What was the gift (Good News, NIV) or promise (KJ, RSV, Beck) they were to wait around for? (vs 5b)

b. How long would they have to wait for this? (vs 5b)

6a. Read vss 6-11. What event is described here? (See section heading in the Good News).

b. Where did this take place? (See 1:12a)

7. What did Jesus' followers think or hope He was going to do at this time? (vs 6)

8a. To what event did Jesus point them again? (vs 8a)

 b. What did He say would happen to them when this happened?

   1. (vs 8a)

   2. (vs 8b, as far as "witnesses", KJ, RSV, NIV; "Me" Good News, Beck)

 c. Where were they to go to do this? (vs 8c)

   1.

   2.

   3.

9. What happened after He said this?

   1. (vs 9a)

   2. (vs 9b)

10. What happened when Jesus' followers were staring up into the sky? (vs 10a)

11a. What question did one of these "men" ask them? (vs 11a)

  b. What announcement did he make then? (vs 11b)

12. Read vss 12-14. Where did Jesus' followers go now?

   1. (vs 12a)

   2. (vs 13a)

13a. Who else beside the eleven apostles were members of the group? (vs 14)

   1.

   2.

   3. (See Mark 6:3)

b. What was the one activity Luke mentions here? (vs 14)

14a. Read vss 15-26. What name did the men of the group choose for themselves? (vs 16a, compare Matt. 23:8)

b. How large a group was it? (vs 15b).

15a. What did Peter talk to the group about on this day?

    1. (vs 16b-17, briefly)

    2. (vss 21-22, briefly, esp. 22b)

b. What had happened to this man? (vs 18b, briefly)

16a. Whom did the group nominate? (vs 23)

b. Which one was elected? (vs 26)

Chapter 2

17a. Read vss 1-4. What festival was being celebrated now? (This was an annual spring harvest festival celebrated 50 (pentecost) days after the Passover, and every male Israelite was required to go to Jerusalem if possible).

b. What information does vs 1b give us? (Compare 1:13)

18. What happened that morning?

    1. (vs 2a)

    2. (vs 2b)

    3. (vs 3)

    4. (vs 4a)

    5. (vs 4b)

    6. (vs 4c)

4

19. Read vss 5-13. What two things are mentioned about the Jews living in Jerusalem? (vs 5)

    1.

    2.

20. What happened when the people heard all this talking (sound)? (vs 6)

    1.

    2.

    3.

21a. What was the reaction of the people? (vs 7a)

  b. Why?

    1. (vs 7b)

    2. (vs 8)

22. How many different nations and languages are listed here? (vss 9-11)

23. What were all of Jesus' followers talking about? (vs 11, last clause).

24. Read vss 14-41. Who was it who delivered the sermon to the crowd? (vs 14a)

25. How did he explain what had happened?

    1. (vs 16)

    2. (vss 17a and 18)

26a. Whom did he begin to talk about then? (vs 22a)

  b. What did he say about Him? (vs 22a, Good News, KJ, RSV, NIV)

  c. What were His credentials? (vs 22b)

27. What did Peter say had happened to Him? (vs 23b)

28a. What had God done then? (vs 24a)

  b. What thought did Peter add in vs 32b? (compare 1:8)

29. What did Peter say had happened then?

    1. (vs 33a)

    2. (vs 33b)

    3. (vs 33c, compare 2:4a)

30. What should the people realize from all this? (vs 36, esp. in the Good News)

31a. What was the effect of Peter's sermon on the people? (vs 37a)

  b. What did they say? (vs 37b)

32. What did Peter tell them they must do? (vs 38a)

    1.

    2.

33. What would happen to them if they did this?

    1. (vs 38b)

    2. (vs 38c)

34. For whom was this salvation intended? (vs 39)

    1.

    2.

    3.

35. How many people were brought to faith that day? (vs 41)

36. Read vss 42-47. How does Luke describe their activities?

   1. (vs 42)

   2. (vs 42)

   3. (vs 42)

   4. (vs 42)

   5. (vs 44)

   6. (vs 44)

   7. (vs 45)

   8. (vs 46a)

   9. (vs 46b)

37. What further information is added in vs 43a?

38. How does Luke explain the growth of the early Church? (vs 47b, compare Matt. 16:18b)

LESSON 2 - ACTS 3-4:31

Jesus Continues to Work Miracles through His Apostles

Fall, 29 A.D.

Chapter 3

1a. Read vss 1-10. Where did Peter and John go on this day? (vs 1a)

b. Why did they go there? (vs 1b)

2a. What was the matter with the man they met there? (vs 2a)

b. How did this man make a living? (vs 2b)

c. Where was his regular place of "business"? (vs 2b, see map)

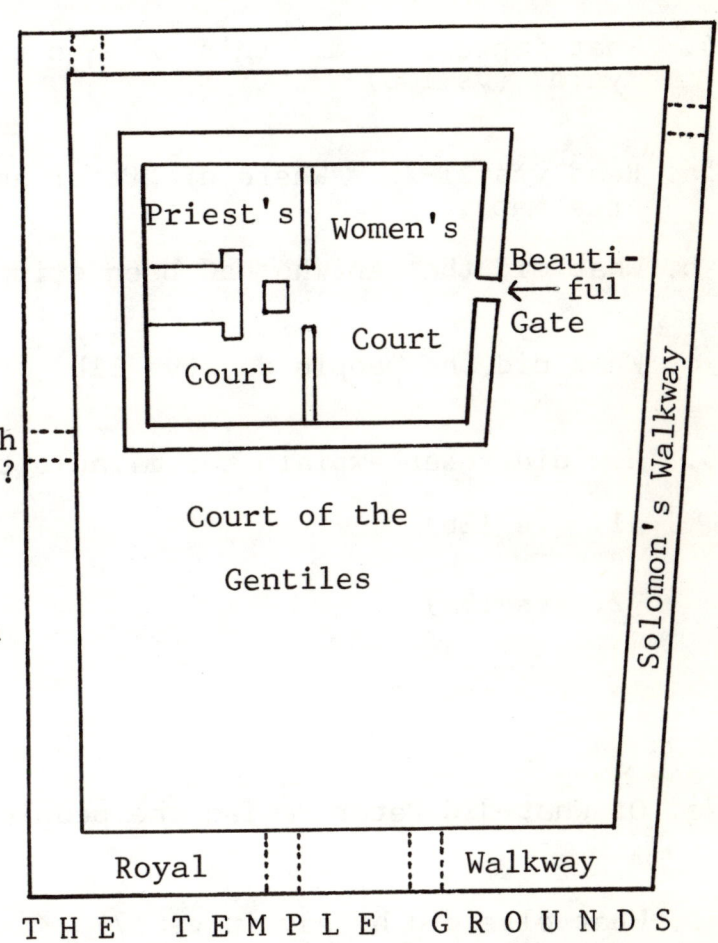

3a. What did Peter say to this man when he asked them for money?

   1. (vs 6a)

   2. (vs 6b)

b. What did he tell the man to do? (vs 6c)

c. What did Peter do then? (vs 7a)

d. What happened when he did this?

   1. (vs 7b)

   2. (vs 8a)

3. (vs 8a)

4. (vs 8b)

4. What impression did this make on the people in the Temple-yard? (vs 10b)

5a. Read vss 11-26. Where did Peter and John go then? (vs 11b, see map).

 b. What did the man who had been crippled do? (vs 11a)

 c. What did the people do? (vs 11b)

6. How did Peter explain the miracle to the people?

   1. (vs 12b)

   2. (vs 13a)

   3. (vs 16b)

7a. Of what did Peter remind the people? (vss 13b and 15a)

 b. What else did he say in vs 17?

 c. How did Peter explain their actions? (vs 18, briefly)

8a. What did Peter tell them they must do? (vs 19a)

 b. What would happen if they did so? (vs 19b)

9a. Who was the prophet Moses was speaking about in vs 22a?

 b. What else did Peter tell the people they must do? (vs 22b)

 c. What warning did he give them? (vs 23)

10a. What did Peter call Jesus in vs 26a? (Good News, NIV, RSV, Beck)

   b. Of what did Peter remind the people in vs 26b? (Compare Rom. 1:16b)

Chapter 4

11. Read vss 1-4. Who joined the crowd at this point? (vs 1)

   1.

   2.

   3.

12a. How does Luke describe their feelings? (vs 2a)

   b. Why? (vs 2)

   1.

   2.

13. What did they do? (vs 3)

   1.

   2.

14. What information does Luke give about the rest of the crowd? (vs 4a)

15. How large was the group of believers now? (vs 4b)

16a. Read vss 5-22. What happened the next morning? (vs 5)

   b. Who else was there? (vs 6)

17a. What did they do? (vs 7a)

   b. What did they want to know? (vs 7b)

18. What was Peter's answer? (vss 8-10, especially vs 10)

19a. What did Peter say the leaders of Israel had done? (vs 10)

   b. And what had God done? (vs 10)

20. What passage of Scripture did Peter quote as one which had just been fulfilled, and which proved that Jesus was the Messiah, the promised Savior? (See footnote at vs 11, Good News, NIV, RSV)

21. What other important thing did Peter tell them? (vs 12)

22a. What was the reaction of the Council to this speech? (vs 13a)

   b. Why? (vs 13a)

   c. What did they realize was the probable cause of their courage? (vs 13b)

23. Why didn't they offer any argument or reply to Peter? (vs 14)

24. What did they do when Peter finished? (vs 15)

   1.

   2.

25a. What was the problem they were discussing? (vs 16a)

   b. What was their main difficulty? (vs 16b)

   1.

   2.

26a. What was their aim or goal? (vs 17a)

b. What did they decide to do? (vs 17b)

27. What did they tell Peter and John? (vs 18)

28. What did Peter and John reply?

    1. (vs 19)

    2. (vs 20)

29a. What happened then? (vs 21a)

    1.

    2.

b. Why did they let them go without any punishment? (vs 21b)

c. How old was the man who had been healed? (vs 22)

30. Read vss 23-31. What did Peter and John do when they were released? (vs 23)

    1.

    2.

31a. What did the others in the group do when they had heard about all this? (vs 24a)

b. What were the opening thoughts of their prayer?

    1. (vs 24b)

    2. (vs 25)

c. What Old Testament passage did they quote? (See footnote at vss 25b-26, Good News, RSV, NIV)

32a. Whom did they say had joined forces against Jesus? (vs 27)

    1.

2.

3.

4.

b. What did they say about all this? (vs 28)

33a. What did they ask God to give them? (vs 29)

b. What did they ask God to do? (vs 30, Good News, NIV)

34. What happened after their prayer? (vs 31)

1.

2.

3.

LESSON 3 - ACTS 4:32-5:42

Jesus Causes His Church to Grow and Fills His Followers with Zeal

30 A.D.

Chapter 4:32-37

1a. What does Luke say about all of Jesus' followers there in Jerusalem? (vs 32a)

b. What does this mean? (vs 32a, see Good News, 2nd sentence, 1st phrase)

2a. How did this perfect oneness show itself? (vs 32b)

b. How did they do this?

   1. (vs 34b)

   2. (vs 35a)

   3. (vs 35b)

c. What was the result of this? (vs 34a)

3a. What was the name of the man who is given as an example of this generous spirit? (vs 36)

b. By what other name was he also known?

c. What did he do? (vs 37)

4. What was the one thing the apostles kept on talking about? (vs 33a)

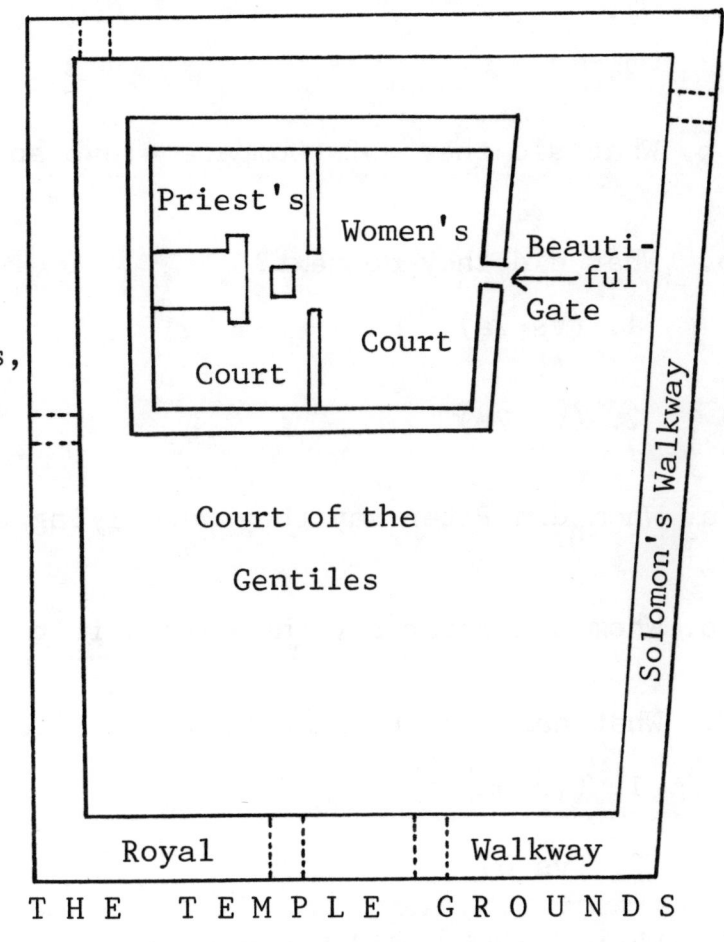
THE TEMPLE GROUNDS

Chapter 5

5a. Read vss 1-11. What were the names of the two people mentioned in vs 1?

    1.

    2.

b. What did they do? (Compare 4:34b and 36-37)

6. What did they do next?

    1. (vs 2a)

    2. (vs 2b)

7a. Whom did Peter say they were lying to? (vs 3a)

b. Whom did Peter say the Holy Spirit was? (vs 4c)

8. What happened to Ananias while Peter was talking to him?

    1. (vs 5a)

    2. (vs 6)

9a. What question did Peter ask Sapphira later? (vs 8b)

b. What was her answer? (vs 8c)

10. What happened then?

    1. (vs 10a)

    2. (vs 10b)

11. What effect did this have on the others? (vs 11)

12a. Read vss 12-16. Where did the believers meet together each day? (vs 12b, see map of the Temple)

b. What did Jesus continue to do through the apostles at this time? (vs 12a)

13. What effect did this have on the people of the city?

    1. (vs 13b)

    2. (vs 14)

    3. (vs 15)

14. What else does Luke tell us in vs 16?

    1. (vs 16a)

    2. (vs 16b)

    3. (vs 16c)

15a. Read vss 17-42. What group of people came to see the apostles now? (vs 17a)

  b. Who made up this group? (vs 17a)

  c. What did they do? (vs 18)

16a. What did the Lord do about this? (vs 19)

  b. What did the angel tell Peter and John to do? (vs 20)

17. What did Annas and the Sadducees do the next morning?

    1. (vs 21b)

    2. (vs 21c)

18. What happened when the officers arrived at the jail? (vs 22a)

16

19. How did the Chief of Police and the priests feel when they heard this? (vs 24)

20. What news did they hear next? (vs 25)

21a. What happened then? (vs 26a)

   b. What was unusual about this arrest? (vs 26b)

   c. Why? (vs 26c)

22a. What happened when Peter and John were brought into the meeting? (vs 27b, Good News)

   b. What did he say to them?

      1. (vs 28a)

      2. (vs 28b)

      3. (vs 28c)

23. What did Peter answer?

      1. (vs 29)

      2. (vs 30)

      3. (vs 31a)

24. What did Peter say Jesus could give the people of Israel?

      1. (vs 31b)

      2. (vs 31c)

25. What did he say about the things he had just told them?

    1. (vs 32a)

    2. (vs 32b)

26. What effect did Peter's words have on the members of the Sanhedrin?

    1. (vs 33a)

    2. (vs 33b)

27a. What was the name of the man who spoke up now? (vs 34a)

  b. What does Luke tell us about this man?

    1. (vs 34a)

    2. (vs 34b)

    3. (vs 34c)

28. What did he tell the Sanhedrin to do first? (vs 34)

29. Then what warning did he give the others? (vs 35)

30a. What two examples did he give from recent history?

    1. (vs 36)

    2. (vs 37)

  b. What happened to both these men? (vss 36-37)

  c. What happened to all their followers? (vss 36-37)

31a. What did Gamaliel advise the Sanhedrin to do? (vs 38a)

b. Why?

    1. (vs 38b)

    2. (vs 39a)

32. What was he trying to keep them from doing? (vs 39b)

33. What did the Sanhedrin finally do?

    1. (vs 40a)

    2. (vs 40b)

    3. (vs 40c)

    4. (vs 40d)

34a. How did Peter and John feel when they left the meeting? (vs 41a)

  b. Why? (vs 41b)

35a. How does Luke describe the activities of the apostles after this? (vs 42b, Good News, NIV)

  b. Where did they do this? (vs 42a)

LESSON 4 - ACTS 6-8:2

The Believers Elect Seven Men to Help the Apostles,
The Story of Stephen
32-33, A.D.

Review

1a. Read 4:32-37. Where did the early Christians get the money to provide food and the other necessary things for the poor members of their group? (vss 34-35a)

 b. Who was in charge of passing out the food and money? (vs 35b)

Chapter 6

2. Read vss 1-7. What information does Luke give in vs 1a?

3a. What problem developed at this time? (vs 1b)

 b. Why? (vs 1c, compare 4:35)

4a. What did the twelve apostles do first? (vs 2a)

 b. What did they say? (vs 2b, Good News, RSV)

5a. Read their suggestion in vs 3. How many men did they say should be chosen?

 b. What kind of men should they be?

   1.

   2.

   3.

 c. What should then be done? (vs 3)

 d. What did the apostles say about themselves? (vs 4)

6a. How did this suggestion sound to the rest of the group? (vs 5a)

 b. Whom did they elect?

    1.   5.

    2.   6.

    3.   7.

    4.

 c. What did they do after they elected them? (vs 6a)

 d. What did the apostles do? (vs 6b)

7. What information does Luke give us in vs 7?

    1.

    2.

    3.

8a. Read vss 8-15. How is Stephen described in vs 8a?

 b. What else does Luke tell us about him? (vs 8b)

9a. As time went along, what happened to him? (vs 9, first and last phrases, briefly)

 b. What was the result of this argument? (vs 10)

10. What did these men do next? (vs 11, Good News, Beck)

11. What was the result of all this talk?

    1. (vs 12a)

    2. (vs 12b)

12a. What happened next? (vs 13, first phrase)

  b. What accusations did these men bring against Stephen?

    1. (vs 13b)

    2. (vs 14)

13. As the members of the Sanhedrin looked at Stephen, what did they see? (vs 15)

Chapter 7

14. Read vss 1-8. What did the Head Priest say after the witnesses finished? (vs 1)

15a. Where did Stephen begin his defense? (vs 2)

  When...

  b. What did God say? (vs 3, Compare Gen. 12:1, RSV, NIV, Beck, Good News)

    1.

    2.

16. What did Abraham do?

    1. (vs 4a)

    2. (vs 4b)

17a. What promise did God make to Abraham? (vs 5b)

  b. What was unusual about this promise? (vs 5c)

18. What else did God tell Abraham?

    1. (vs 6a)

2. (vs 6b)

3. (vs 6c)

4. (vs 7b)

19. How did Stephen summarize the story of Abraham's family?

1. (vs 8b)

2. (vs 8d)

3. (vs 8e)

20a. Read vss 9-10. Whom did Stephen talk about in this section?

b. What were the main features of this story?

1. (vs 9a)

2. (vss 9b-10a)

3. (vs 10b)

21. Read vss 11-16. Summarize what happened in this section.

1. (vs 11a)

2. (vs 11b)

3. (vs 12)

4. (vs 13a)

5. (vss 14-15a)

22. Read vss 17-19. Summarize this part of the history of Israel.

1. (vs 17b)

2. (vs 18)

3. (vs 19)

23. Read vss 20-29. Summarize this section briefly.

   1. (vs 20a)

   2. (vs 21)

   3. (vs 23)

   4. (vs 25a)

   5. (vs 25, last phrase)

   6. (vs 29)

24a. Read vss 30-35. What happened one day in the desert? (vs 30)

  b. What did God tell Moses?

   1. (vs 34a)

   2. (vs 34b)

   3. (vs 34c)

25. Read vss 36-45. Summarize this section briefly.

   1. (vs 36)

   2. (vs 38b-c)

   3. (vs 41a)

   4. (vs 44a)

26a. Read vss 46-50. Who was it who built the Temple? (vs 47)

  b. Where did Stephen say God lives?

   1. (vs 48)

   2. (vs 49a)

27. Read vss 51-53. What did Stephen then say to the Jewish leaders?

    1. (vs 51a, first phrase)

    2. (rest of 51a, Beck, Good News)

    3. (vs 51b)

    4. (vs 52a)

    5. (vs 52b)

    6. (vs 52c)

    7. (vs 53)

28. Read vss 54-8:1a. What effects did Stephen's speech have on the members of the Sanhedrin? (vs 54)

29a. What did Stephen see at this time?

  b. What did he say?

30a. What did the members of the Sanhedrin do then? (vs 58)

  b. Who was in charge of the execution? (vs 58c)

31a. What did Stephen say? (vs 60a)

  b. What happened then? (vs 60b)

  c. How does this story end?

    1. (8:2a)

    2. (8:2b)

LESSON 5 - ACTS 8

Jesus' Enemies' Plan to Destroy the Church Causes the Good News to Spread

33-34 A.D.

Chapter 8

1a. Read vss 1b and 3. What happened right after Stephen's death? (vs 1b)

b. What happened as the result of this? (vs 1c)

c. What about the apostles? (vs 1d)

2a. Who was the leader of this effort to destroy the church? (vs 3a)

b. How does Luke describe his actions? (vs 3b)

3. Read vss 4-8. What good effect did this persecution have? (vs 4, compare 1:8)

4a. To whom are we introduced in vs 5a?

b. Where did he go? (vs 5a, locate on the map)

5. Why did the Samaritans receive his message so readily? (vss 6-7)

6a. Read vss 9-13. Whom did Philip meet there in Samaria? (vs 9a)

b. What had this man been doing there? (vs 9b)

   1.

   2.

   3.

7a. How had the people of Samaria received this man? (vs 10c)

b. Why? (vs 11)

8. What was the result of Philip's preaching? (vs 12b)

9a. Who was included in the group of new believers there? (vs 13a)

  b. What did he do after his baptism? (vs 13b)

  c. What was it that particularly impressed him? (vs 13c)

10. Read vss 14-25. What did the apostles do when they heard about Philip's work in Samaria? (vs 14)

11a. What did they do when they arrived? (vs 15)

  b. Why? (vs 16a)

12. What happened when Peter & John put their hands on them? (vs 17)

13a. What did Simon do when he saw this? (vs 18)

  b. What did he say to Peter and John? (vs 19)

14a. What did Peter say to him? (vs 20a, Good News)

  b. Why? (vs 20b)

15a. What else did Peter tell him? (vs 21a)

  b. Why? (vs 21b)

16. What did Peter say he must do?

    1. (vs 22a)

    2. (vs 22b)

17. What did Peter say about Simon? (vs 23, NIV, Good News)

18. What did Simon reply? (vs 24)

19. What did Peter and John do next? (vs 25a)

20a. What did they do after they finished? (vs 25b)

   b. What did they do on the way? (vs 25c)

21. Read vss 26-40. Where did Jesus tell Philip to go at this time? (vs 26, locate on your map)

22a. Who else was travelling on that road that day? (vs 27a)

   b. Where was this man from? (vs 27a)

   c. What position did he hold there? (vs 27b)

   d. How would the Jews of that time look upon this man? (See Gal. 2:15)

   e. How did the Jews feel about such people? (See Acts 11:3)

   f. Where had this man just been? (vs 27c)

   g. Why had he gone there? (vs 27c)

23a. Where was he going now? (vs 28a)

   b. What was he doing? (vs 28b)

24. What instructions did the Holy Spirit give Philip? (vs 29)

25a. What happened when Philip got to the chariot? (vs 30a)

b. What did he say to the man? (vs 30b)

26a. What did the man answer? (vs 31a)

  b. What did he ask Philip to do? (vs 31b)

27a. What part of Isaiah was the man reading? (vss 32-33, NIV, RSV, Beck, Good News, footnotes)

  b. What question did he ask Philip? (vs 34)

28. What did Philip do then? (vs 35)

29a. What happened some time after Philip finished his story? (vs 36a)

  b. What did the man say to Philip? (vs 36b)

    1.

    2.

30. What happened then?

    1. (vs 38a)

    2. (vs 38b)

    3. (vs 38c)

31. What happened as soon as they stepped up out of the water?

    1. (vs 39a)

    2. (vs 39b)

32. What did the man do? (vs 39c)

33a. Where did Philip find himself next? (vs 40a, locate on your map)

  b. What did he do then? (vs 40b, locate on your map)

LESSON 6 - ACTS 9:1-31

Jesus Calls Saul to be His Follower

35-37 A.D.

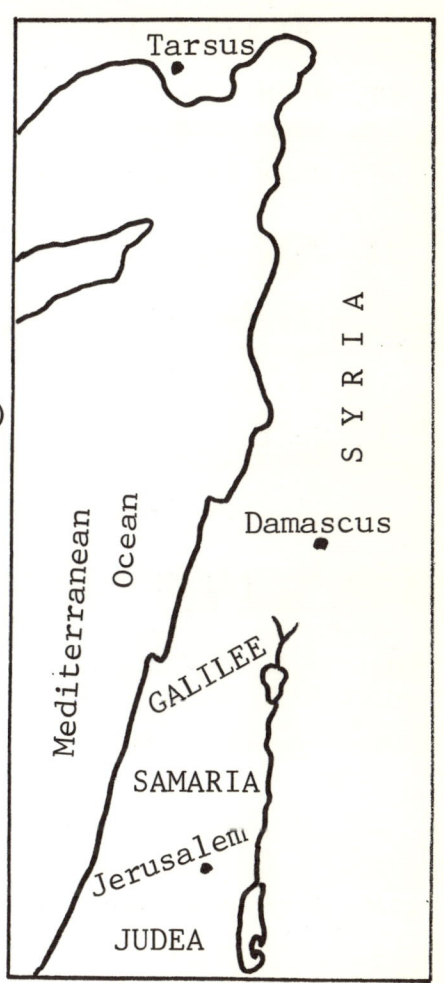

Review

1. Read 8:1b-3 again. What does this section tell about? (vs 3a)

Chapter 9

2a. What was going on at this time? (vs 1a)

 b. Where did Saul decide to go now? (vs 2a)

 c. What did he do therefore? (vss 1b-2a)

 d. What was he planning to do? (vs 2b)

 e. What was the Christian faith called at this time? (vs 2b, Good News, NIV)

3. Read vss 3-9. What happened when Saul got close to Damascus? (vs 3b)

4a. What did Saul do? (vs 4a)

 b. What happened then? (vs 4b)

5a. What did Saul answer? (vs 5a)

 b. What did the voice answer? (vs 5b)

 c. What instructions did He give Saul? (vs 6)

    1.

    2.

6a. What happened when Saul stood up? (vs 8a)

 b. What did his friends do, therefore? (vs 8b)

7. What happened when Saul arrived in the city?

   1. (vs 9a)

   2. (vs 9b)

8a. Read vss 10-16. What information does Luke give us in vs 10a?

  b. What happened to this man one day? (vs 10b)

9a. What instructions did Jesus then give to Ananias?

   1. (vs 11a)

   2. (vs 11b)

  b. What did He tell Ananias about Saul?

   1. (vs 11c)

   2. (vs 12)

10. What did Ananias reply?

   1. (vs 13)

   2. (vs 14)

11a. What did Ananias call the Christians living in Jerusalem? (vs 13b, KJ, RSV, NIV)

  b. What does this word mean? (See Good News, footnote)

12a. What did the Lord say about Saul? (vs 15)

  b. What else did He say about Saul? (vs 16)

13. Read vss 17-25. What did Ananias say to Saul when he found him? (vs 17)

14. What happened then?

   1. (vs 18a)

   2. (vs 18b)

   3. (vs 19a)

15a. What did Saul do now? (vs 19b)

   b. What did he begin to do right away? (vs 20a)

   c. What was the main point of his preaching? (vs 20b)

16a. What was the reaction of the people who heard him? (vs 21a)

   b. What did they say?

      1. (vs 21a)

      2. (vs 21b)

17a. What information does Luke add in vs 22a?

   b. What was Saul trying to prove to the Jews who were living in Damascus? (vs 22b)

   c. What effect did his arguments have on them? (vs 22b, Good News)

18a. What happened after Saul had been there quite a long time? (vs 23)

   b. What happened, however, to their plan? (vs 24a)

19a. What were the Jews doing because of their plot? (vs 24b)

   b. How did Saul escape? (vs 25)

20a. Read vss 26-31. Where did Saul go now? (vs 26a)

   b. What did he do when he got there? (vs 26a)

   c. What happened when he did this? (vs 26b)

21a. Who came forward to help Saul? (vs 27a)

b. What did he do?

   1. (vs 27a)

   2. (vs 27b)

   3. (vs 27c)

22. What did Saul do after this?

    1. (vs 28)

    2. (vs 29a, compare 6:1, Good News, Beck, NIV)

23. What did these people do? (vs 29b)

24. What did the brothers do then? (vs 30)

25. What was the result of Saul's conversion? (vs 31a, Good News, NIV)

    1.

    2. (vs 31b)

    3. (vs 31b)

    4. (vs 31b)

LESSON 7 - ACTS 9:32-10:23a

Peter Travels around Judea and Samaria as One of the Apostles
39-40 A.D.

Chapter 9

1a. Read vss 32-35. What was Peter doing at this time? (vs 32a)

  b. What was the name of the town he came to now? (vs 32, locate on the map)

  c. Why did he go there? (vs 32)

2a. Whom did he meet there? (vs 33a)

  b. What was the matter with this man? (vs 33b)

  c. How long had he been crippled? (vs 33b)

3. What did Peter say to him? (vs 34a-b, Good News, RSV)

    1.

    2.

4. What happened? (vs 34c)

5. What effect did this have on the people in town? (vs 35)

6a. Read vss 36-43. To whom does Luke introduce us in vs 36a?

  b. Where did she live? (vs 36a, locate on the map)

  c. How does Luke describe her? (vs 36b, Good News, NIV, Beck)

7a. What happened during this time that Peter was in Lydda? (vs 37a)

  b. What did the believers do? (vs 37b)

8. What did they do next? (vs 38b)

9a. What happened when Peter got there? (vs 39b)

 b. What were all the widows doing? (vs 39c)

10. What did Peter do?

    1. (vs 40a)

    2. (vs 40b)

    3. (vs 40c)

11. What happened? (vs 40d)

12. What effect did this have on the people in town? (vs 42)

    1.

    2.

13. With whom was Peter staying there in Joppa? (vs 43)

Chapter 10

14a. Read vss 1-8. To whom does Luke introduce us in vs 1a?

  b. Where was he living? (vs 1a, locate on the map)

  c. What was his occupation? (vs 1b, Good News, Beck)

15. What else does Luke tell us about him? (vs 2, Good News, RSV)

    1.

    2.

16. What happened to him one day? (vs 3, briefly)

17. What did the angel say to him?

    1. (vs 4c, Good News)

2. (vs 5)

18. What did Cornelius do when the angel left? (vss 7-8, briefly)

19a. Read vss 9-23a. When did the messengers arrive? (vs 9a)

  b. What was Peter doing at this time? (vs 9b)

  c. How was he feeling? (vs 10a)

20a. What happened to Peter while he was praying? (vs 10b, Good News)

  b. What did he see? (vs 11)

21. What was in this big sheet? (vs 12, Good News, RSV, NIV)

     1.

     2.

     3.

22. What did the voice tell Peter to do? (vs 13)

23. What did Peter answer? (vs 14, Good News, NIV)

24. What did the voice reply? (vs 15)

25a. How many times was this scene repeated? (vs 16a)

  b. What happened then? (vs 16b)

26a. What was Peter's reaction to all this? (vs 17a)

  b. What happened while he was thinking about it?

     1. (vs 17)

     2. (vs 18)

27. What did the Holy Spirit say to Peter then?

    1. (vs 19b)

    2. (vs 20a)

    3. (vs 20b)

28. What did the men tell Peter when he came down?

    1. (vs 22a)

    2. (vs 22b, Good News)

    3. (vs 22c, Good News)

29. What did Peter do then? (vs 23a)

LESSON 8 - ACTS 10:23b-11:18

Peter Goes to See a Roman Army Captain in Caesarea
39-40 A.D.

Chapter 10

1a. Read vss 23b-33. What did Peter do the next day? (vs 23b)

 b. Who else went along with him? (vs 23b)

 c. How long did it take to get there? (vs 24a)

2. What had Cornelius done to prepare for Peter's arrival? (vs 24b)

3. What did Cornelius do as Peter was about to enter the house? (vs 25, Good News, Beck)

4a. What did Peter do then? (vs 26a)

 b. What did Peter say to him? (vs 26b, Good News)

5a. What did Peter find when he got in the house? (vs 27)

 b. What did Peter say to them?

   1. (vs 28a)

   2. (vs 28b)

   3. (vs 29a)

   4. (vs 29b)

6. What did Cornelius answer?

   1. (vs 30a, Good News, Beck)

   2. (vs 30b)

7. What did Cornelius say the "man" had told him?

   1. (vs 31)

   2. (vs 32)

   3. (vs 33a, Good News)

   4. (vs 33b)

8. Read vss 34-43. How did Peter begin his speech?

   1. (vs 34)

   2. (vs 35)

9. What did Peter talk about next?

   1. (vs 36)

   2. (vs 37)

   3. (vs 38a)

   4. (vs 38b)

10. What did Peter say about himself and the other apostles? (vs 39a)

11. What two things about Jesus did he mention specifically?

    1. (vs 39b)

    2. (vs 40)

12. Who was it who actually saw Jesus after His resurrection? (vs 41b)

13. What orders had they received from Jesus? (vs 42, Good News)

14. What did Peter say about Jesus then? (vs 43)

15. Read vss 44-48. What happened while Peter was talking? (vs 44)

16a. What effect did this have on the Jewish believers who had come with Peter? (vs 45a)

　b. Why? (vs 45b, see note in the Good News)

17. How did they know that God had poured out His Holy Spirit on Cornelius and his friends? (vs 46)

18a. Read vss 47-48. What did Peter say when he saw this? (vs 47)

　　　1.

　　　2.

　b. What did he do then? (vs 48a)

19. What did they ask Peter to do after this? (vs 48b)

Chapter 11

20. Read vss 1-18. What information does Luke record in vs 1?

21a. What happened, therefore, when Peter came back to Jerusalem? (vs 2)

　b. What did they say? (vs 3)

22a. What did Peter do then? (vs 4)

　b. Summarize briefly what he told them.

　　　1. (vss 5-6)

　　　2. (vs 7)

3. (vs 8)

4. (vs 9)

5. (vs 10)

6. (vs 11)

7. (vs 12a)

8. (vs 12b)

23. How did Peter summarize Cornelius' message? (vs 13-14, briefly)

24. What did Peter tell them about then? (vs 15)

25. How did Peter describe his feelings and thoughts at this point?

   1. (vs 16)

   2. (vs 17)

26. What effect did this speech have on those who had criticized Peter?

   1. (vs 18a)

   2. (vs 18b)

LESSON 9 - ACTS 11:19-12:25

The Good News Reaches Antioch; King Herod Tries to Destroy the Church

40-44 A.D.

Chapter 11

1a. Read vss 19-26. To what event does vs 19a take us back? (See 8:1, 3-4)

b. What information is added in vs 19b? (Locate on your map)

c. What else does Luke tell us in vs 19c?

2a. What happened in Antioch? (vs 20)

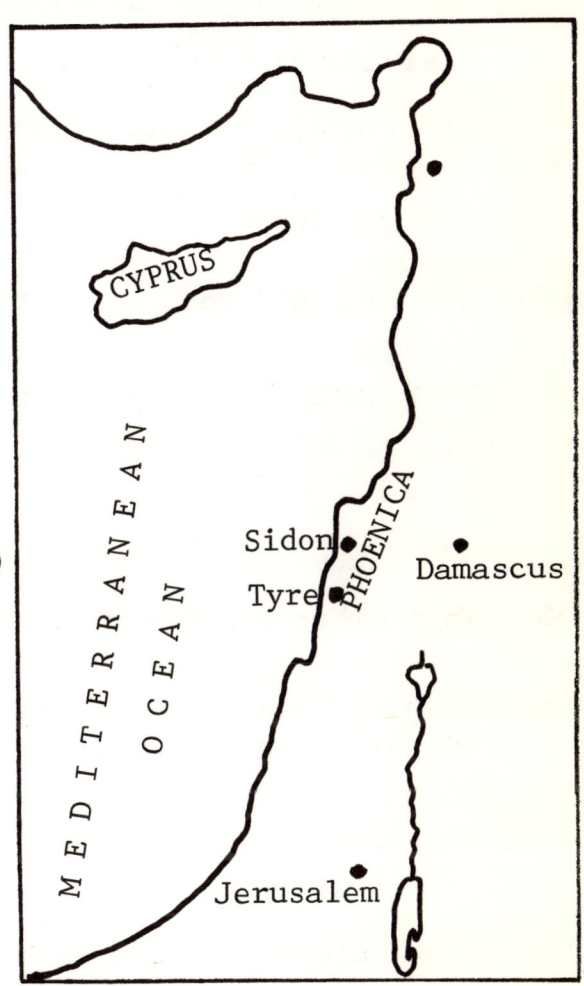

b. Who was working with them? (vs 21a)

c. What were the results of their efforts? (vs 21b)

3a. What did the apostles in Jerusalem do when they heard about this? (vs 22, see Acts 4:36-7 and 9:27)

b. What information about him is given in vs 24a?

   1.

   2.

   3.

4a. How did he feel when he got to Antioch? (vs 23a)

b. Why? (vs 23a, Good News, Beck)

c. What did he do? (vs 23b)

5a. What were the results of his work there? (vs 24b)

   b. Who was it who added these new believers to the group? (vs 24b, compare 2:47)

6. What did Barnabas do next?

   1. (vs 25, compare 9:30)

   2. (vs 26a)

7a. How long did the two of them stay there in Antioch? (vs 26b)

   b. What were they doing during this time? (vs 26b)

      1.

      2.

8. What other new custom also started in Antioch? (vs 26c)

9a. Read vss 27-30. What else happened during this time that Barnabas and Saul were working in Antioch? (vs 27)

   b. What was the name of the one who delivered the message? (vs 28a)

10a. What information did he bring them? (vs 28b)

   b. When did this happen? (vs 28c, see note in the Good News)

11a. What did the believers decide to do about this? (vs 29b)

   b. What rule did each of them use to determine how much to give? (vs 29a)

12. Whom did they send as their ambassadors to bring their gift? (vs 30)

<u>Chapter 12</u>

13a. Read vss 1-5. What happened next? (vs 1)

   b. Which Herod was this? (See note in the Good News)

14a. Who was one of his first victims? (vs 2)

  b. What did he do to him? (vs 2)

15a. What did Herod do next? (vs 3a)

  b. Why? (vs 3a)

16. When did this happen? (vs 3b, see note at Luke 22:1 in the Good News)

17. What did he do to Peter after he arrested him? (vs 4a)

    1.

    2.

18. What was he planning to do? (vs 4b)

19. What was the situation, then, during the Passover? (vs 5)

    1.

    2.

20a. Read vss 6-19. When did all this take place? (vs 6a)

  b. What was the situation when the story begins? (vs 6)

    1.

    2.

    3.

21a. What happened first? (vs 7a)

    1.

    2.

  b. What did the angel do? (vs 7b)

  c. What did he say to Peter? (vs 7c)

  d. What happened then? (vs 7d)

43

22a. What did the angel say next? (vs 8a)

   b. What did he say after Peter had done so? (vs 8b)

23a. What happened then? (vs 9a)

   b. What was Peter's mental condition at this time? (vs 9b)

   c. What did he think was happening? (vs 9c, Good News)

24a. What did they do now? (vs 10a)

   b. Where did they come to then? (vs 10b)

   c. What happened when they got there? (vs 10c)

   d. What happened after they had walked a block? (vs 10d)

25a. What had happened to Peter when he got outside? (vs 11a, Good News)

   b. What did he say to himself? (vs 11b)

26a. Where did he go now? (vs 12a)

   b. What was going on there? (vs 12b)

27a. What happened when Peter knocked on the door of the outside gate? (vs 13)

   b. What did she do when she came to the door?

      1. (vs 14a)

      2. (vs 14b)

28a. What did she tell the people in the house? (vs 14c)

   b. How did they receive this news? (vs 15a and c)

29a. What was Peter doing all this time? (vs 16a)

  b. What happened when they opened the door? (vs 16b)

30a. What did Peter do then?

    1. (vs 17a)

    2. (vs 17b)

  b. What instructions did he give them? (vs 17c)

  c. Who was this James? (See Mark 6:3 and I Cor. 15:7 and the note in the Good News)

31. What did Peter do then? (vs 17d)

32a. What happened the next morning? (vs 18, Good News)

  b. What did Herod do?

    1. (vs 19a)

    2. (vs 19b)

    3. (vs 19c)

    4. (vs 19d)

33a. Read vss 20-25. What was going on at this time? (vs 20a, locate on your map)

  b. What did these people from Tyre and Sidon do now? (vs 20b)

34. What did they want? (vs 20c)

35. What happened on the appointed day? (vs 21)

36. What did the people of Tyre and Sidon say when he finished? (vs 22)

37a. What happened then? (vs 23a, Good News, Beck, RSV)

   b. Why? (vs 23b)

   c. What was Herod's punishment? (vs 23c)

38. What happened after this? (vs 24)

39. What did Barnabas and Saul do when they finished their errand to Jerusalem? (vs 25)

    1.

    2.

LESSON 10 - JAMES

James Writes to the Jewish Christians

45-50 A.D.

Chapter 1 (12:24 probably pictures the time in which this letter was sent)

1a. Who wrote this letter?

  b. To whom did Peter send the news of his release from jail? (Acts 12:17)

  c. To whom did Paul go to give a report of his third trip? (Acts 21:18)

  d. What did Paul call James in Galatians 2:9?

  e. Who were the other two men whom he mentions in Gal. 2:9?

  f. Who were the two men from Jerusalem who spoke at the big meeting of the church described in Acts 15:6-21?

  g. From all these incidents (b-f) what would we say about James' position or standing in the church in Jerusalem?

  h. Which James was it who was spoken about in all these questions? (See note at Acts 12:17, Good News, question 30c, last lesson)

  i. How does he introduce himself to his readers in this letter? (vs 1a)

2a. To whom did he write his letter? (vs 1b, first 4 words)

  b. Who would the "twelve tribes" refer to?

  c. Where were these people living? (See NIV, Beck, or "disperse" in the dictionary)

3a. Read vss 2-4. What does vs 2 tell us about these people? (NIV, RSV, Beck)

  b. How did James say they should look at their troubles? (vs 2a)

  c. Why? (vs 3, NIV, RSV)

4a. What did James say about perseverance or patience in 4a?

  b. What will then be the final result? (vs 4b)

5a. Read vss 5-8. What should a Christian do if he or she lacks wisdom? (vs 5a)

b. What is the promised result if he does this? (vs 5b)

6. What is the one necessary requirement, however, when we pray to God? (vs 6a, see Mark 11:23-24)

7a. Read vss 9-11. What does the poor person have to boast about? (vs 9)

b. What does the rich person have to boast about? (vs 10a)

c. What will happen to the rich man? (vs 10b)

d. What little story does James use to make this clear to us? (vs 11, briefly)

8a. Read vss 12-15. What general truth does James point out in vs 12a? (Compare vss 2-4 above and Matt. 5:3-10)

b. Why? (vs 12b)

9a. Where do our temptations to do evil things come from? (vs 14)

b. What mistaken idea must we avoid? (vs 13)

c. How does James describe the growth and development of sin in our lives?

    1. (vs 15a)

    2. (vs 15b)

10. Read vss 16-18. Where do all good things come from? (vs 17)

11a. What kind of birth is James talking about in vs 18a? (See I Peter 1:3 and 1:23, John 3:3-5)

b. What is the ultimate cause of our new birth? (vs 18a)

c. What error is James correcting here? (See Ephesians 2:8-9, II Timothy 1:9, Titus 3:5)

d. How is the new birth effected? (vs 18a)

e. What is God's purpose in this? (vs 18b)

12a. Read vss 19-21. What does James say we should be quick to do? (vs 19)

  b. What else does he say we should do?

   1. (vs 21a)

   2. (vs 21b, compare vss 22-25)

13. How does James describe a truly Christian life?

   1. (vs 26)

   2. (vs 27a)

   3. (vs 27b)

Chapter 2

14. Read vss 1-9. What sin does James warn his readers about in this section? (vss 1b and 9a, Beck)

15. In the story that James uses (vss 2-3), how did the people illustrate what James meant? (briefly)

16. How has God treated the poor people? (vs 5, see Matt. 5:3)

17. Which commandment must we follow to avoid this sin? (vs 8)

18. Read vss 10-13. What does James say here about keeping God's Law? (vs 10)

19. What does James refer to when he talks about the law that sets us free? (vs 12, compare 1:25 in Beck and Eph. 1:13a)

20a. Read vss 14-26. What does James have to say about our faith? (vss 17 and 26, see Gal. 5:6, Matt. 7:17, John 15:5)

  b. What word picture does he use to illustrate this? (vs 26b)

Chapter 3

21. Read vss 1-12. What kind of sins is James talking about here? (vss 2b, 6, 8a, 9b)

22. What does James say about the tongue in vs 6? (NIV, RSV)

    1.

    2.

    3.

    4.

    5.

23. What else does he say about it in vs 8?

24. What example does he give of the tongue's sinfulness? (vs 9)

    1.

    2.

25. How does he sum up this paragraph? (vs 2b)

26. Read vss 13-18. How can a person show that he or she is truly wise and understanding? (vs 13, NIV)

    1.

    2.

27. What are the marks of heavenly wisdom? (vs 17, NIV)
    1.

    2.

    3.

    4.

    5.

    6.

    7. (KJ, Beck)

Chapter 4

28. Read vss 1-10. What is James warning us against here? (vs 4a)

29. Where do all our fights and quarrels come from? (vs 1, Beck)

30. How does he describe the life of the typical man or woman?

    1. (vs 2a)

    2. (vs 2b)

    3. (vs 2c)

31. What does he say about this kind of life?

    1. (vs 2d, NIV)

    2. (vs 3)

32. How does James sum up this section in vs 4b?

33. What is the remedy for our problem?

    1. (vs 7a)

    2. (vs 7b)

    3. (vs 8a)

    4. (vs 8b)

    5. (vs 9a)

    6. (vs 10)

34. Read vss 11-12. What sin does James warn against here? (vs 11a, Beck, RSV)

35. Read vss 13-17. What sin does he warn against here? (vs 16)

36a. What example does he give? (vs 13)

   b. Why is this bragging? (vs 14)

37. How should a Christian make his plans for the future? (vs 15)

38. What does James say about the person who knows what is the right thing to do and fails to do it? (vs 17)

Chapter 5

39. Read vss 1-6. What does James say here to the rich?

    1. (vs 1)

    2. (vs 2)

    3. (vs 3a)

    4. (vs 5a)

    5. (vs 5b)

40a. Read vss 7-12. What advice does James give his readers in vs 7a?

  b. What does he say about the time of Jesus' return? (vss 8b and 9b)

  c. Whom does he refer to as examples of patient suffering? (vs 10)

  d. Whom does he refer to as an example of perseverance? (vs 11)

41. Read vss 13-18. What does James say we should do when we're in trouble? (vs 13c)

42a. What does he say we should do when we get sick? (vs 14a)

  b. What will the church officers do? (vs 14b)

  c. What further promise does he make regarding such prayers? (vs 15)

  d. What special requirement is necessary, however, regarding such prayers? (vs 15)

43a. What does he say about the prayer of a righteous person? (vs 16b)

  b. Whom does he offer as an example of such prayers? (vss 17-18)

44. Read vss 19-20. Of what important truth does James remind us in these closing words? (vs 20)

LESSON 11 - ACTS 13

The Lord Sends Saul (Paul) off on His First Trip

47-48 A.D.

Chapter 13

1. Read vss 1-3. Who were the prophets and teachers in the church in Antioch at this time? (vs 1)

    1.

    2.

    3.

    4.

    5.

2a. What message did the Holy Spirit send them one day? (vs 2)

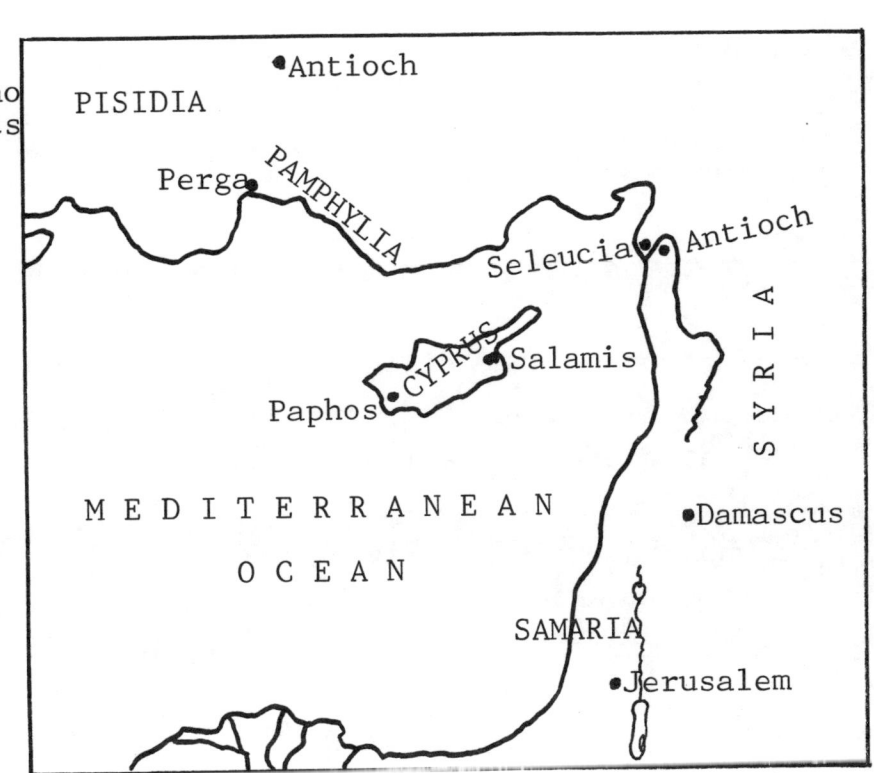

b. What did the people of the congregation do, therefore? (vs 3)

3a. Read vss 4-12. How did Barnabas and Saul begin their trip? (vs 4, locate on your map)

    1.

    2.

b. Who was it who directed their actions? (vs 4a)

4a. What was their first stop? (vs 5a, locate on your map)

b. Where did they go to find people to talk to? (vs 5)

c. How does Luke describe their activity in vs 5?

d. Whom had they taken along as their helper? (vs 5b, see 12:25)

5a. What did Barnabas and Saul do next? (vs 6a)

   b. What was the name of the next city they came to? (vs 6a, locate on your map)

6a. What was the name of the man they met there? (vs 6b)

   b. What was his occupation? (vs 6b, Good News, see note)

   c. What other name did he use? (vs 8a, see 8b in the Good News)

   d. What does Luke call him? (vs 6b)

7a. Whom was this man living with? (vs 7a)

   b. What kind of a man was he? (vs 7b)

   c. What did he do? (vs 7c)

8. What did Elymas try to do? (vs 8c)

9a. What was Saul's Roman name? (vs 9)

   b. What did he call Elymas? (vs 10)

      1.

      2.

   c. What did he accuse Elymas of doing? (vs 10b, Good News, RSV)

10a. What did Paul say the Lord was going to do to Elymas? (vs 11a)

b. What happened when he said this? (vs 11b)

   1.

   2.

11. What effect did this have on the Governor? (vs 12, Good News, Beck)

   1.

   2.

12a. Read vss 13-15. Where did Paul and his friends go now? (vs 13a, locate on your map)

  b. What happened when they got there? (vs 13b)

13a. Where did they go from there? (vs 14a, locate on your map)

  b. What was the first thing they did there? (vs 14b)

14. What message did the officers of the meeting house send to them? (vs 15)

15a. Read vss 16-20a. What was Paul's opening thought? (vs 17a)

  b. Whom did he mean by "our fathers"? (See Gen. 12:1, 26:12, 28:10)

     1.   2.   3.

16. What did Paul talk about then?

    1. (vs 17b)

    2. (vs 17c)

    3. (vs 18)

    4. (vs 19)

17. How long did all this take? (vs 20a)

18. Read vss 20b-25. What did Paul talk about next?

    1. (vs 20b, 20 in KJ)

    2. (vs 21)

    3. (vs 22a)

19a. What did God say about David in vs 22b?

    1.

    2.

  b. What did He say about him in vs 23?

20. What did Paul talk about in vss 24-25? (briefly)

21. Read vss 26-31. For whom was this message of salvation intended? (vs 26)

22. What did Paul tell the people about in vss 27-29?

    1. (vs 27a)

    2. (vs 27b)

    3. (vs 28b)

    4. (vs 29)

23. What did Paul say about the reason Jesus was killed? (vs 28a)

24. What did Paul say happened after Jesus' death?

    1. (vs 30)

    2. (vs 31a)

25. What did Paul say about the apostles who had seen Jesus alive? (vs 31b)

26. Read vss 32-41. What did Paul say about himself and Barnabas? (vs 32)

27. What passage in the Old Testament did Paul refer to as one which spoke about Jesus' resurrection? (vs 33b, see note in Good News, NIV, Beck)

28. What did Paul say about Jesus' resurrection body? (vs 34a, Good News, RSV, Beck)

29. How did Paul sum up his message in vss 38-39?

    1. (vs 38)

    2. (vs 39)

30. What did he say about Moses' Law? (vs 39b)

31. What warning did Paul then give the people? (vss 40-41, briefly)

32a. Read vss 42-45. What happened when the service was over?

    1. (vs 42)

    2. (vs 43a)

  b. What did Paul and Barnabas do? (vs 43b)

33. What happened on the next Sabbath? (vs 44)

34. What did the Jews do when they saw all the other people there?

    1. (vs 45a)

    2. (vs 45b)

    3. (vs 45c, Good News, RSV, Beck)

35. Read vss 46-49. What did Paul and Barnabas say in reply?

   1. (vs 46a)

   2. (vs 46b)

36a. What did Paul call himself in vs 47b?

   b. What did he say his work was? (vs 47c)

37a. How did the gentiles (non-Jews) feel when they heard this? (vs 48a)

   b. What did they say? (vs 48b, Good News)

38. What were the results of Paul's and Barnabas' work in Antioch?

   1. (vs 48c)

   2. (vs 49)

39. Read vss 50-52. What did the Jews do next?

   1. (vs 50a, Good News, Beck)

   2. (vs 50b)

40. What did Paul and Barnabas do then?

   1. (vs 51a, Good News)

   2. (vs 51b)

41. What about the believers there in Antioch? (vs 52)

LESSON 12 - ACTS 14-15:35

Paul and Barnabas Return Home and Go to Jerusalem

48-49 A.D.

Chapter 14

1a. Read vss 1-6a. Where were Paul and Barnabas now? (vs 1a, locate on map)

b. Where did they go first to begin their work? (vs 1a, compare 13:14b)

c. What was the result of their work that day? (vs 1b)

2a. Who was it who stirred up trouble for the apostles? (vs 2a)

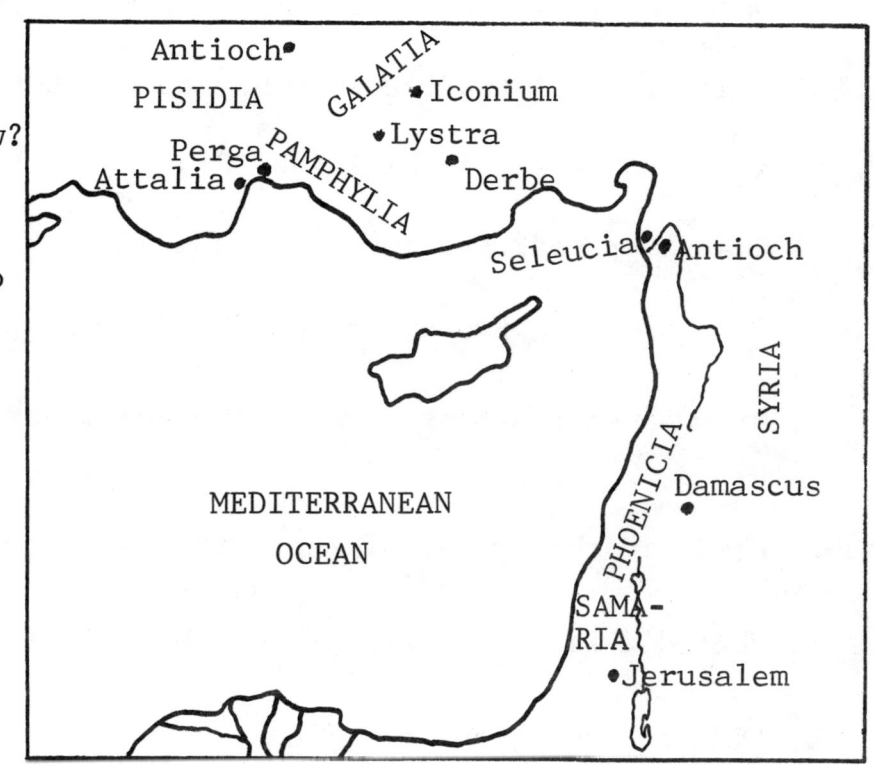

b. What did they do? (vs 2)

3a. What did Paul and Barnabas do then? (vs 3a)

b. How did the Lord help them? (vs 3b)

4. What was the result of their work there? (vs 4)

5a. What happened then? (vs 5)

b. What did the apostles do when they heard of this plot? (vs 6a)

6a. Read vss 6-20. Where did Paul and Barnabas go now? (vs 6b, locate on the map)

b. What did they do there? (vs 7)

7a. Where did this next incident take place? (vs 8a, locate on the map)

   b. Whom did Paul and Barnabas meet there? (vs 8)

   c. What was this man doing as the story begins? (vs 9a)

8a. What did Paul realize when he looked at this man? (vs 9b)

   b. What did he say to him? (vs 10a)

   c. What happened? (vs 10b)

9a. What did the people say when they saw this? (vs 11)

   b. What names did they give to the apostles? (vs 12)

      1. Barnabas -   2. Paul -

10. What did the priest of Zeus do? (vs 13)

11a. What did Paul and Barnabas do then? (vs 14)

   b. What did they say? (vs 15a)

   c. What did they say they had come to do? (vs 15b, Good News, NIV)

12. What was the result of their pleas? (vs 18)

13a. What happened next?

      1. (vs 19a, Good News, NIV, Beck)

      2. (vs 19b)

14. What happened when the believers went out to see Paul? (vs 20a)

15a. Where did Paul and Barnabas go next? (vs 20b, locate on your map)

   b. Read vss 21-28. What happened in Derbe? (vs 21a)

16a. Where did Paul and Barnabas go after this? (vs 21b, locate on your map)

   1.   2.   3.

  b. What did they do in each city? (vs 22a)

  c. What important truth did they tell the people? (vs 22b)

17. What did the apostles do before they left each city?

    1. (vs 23a)

    2. (vs 23b)

18. Where did they go then? (locate on your map)

    1. (vs 24)

    2. (vs 25b)

    3. (vs 26a)

19. What did they do when they returned home?

    1. (vs 27)

    2. (vs 28)

Chapter 15

20a. Read vss 1-2. What happened now? (vs 1a)

  b. What did these men tell the brothers? (vs 1b)

21. What did the brothers decide to do? (vs 2b, briefly)

22. Read vss 3-5. What happened when Paul and Barnabas got to Jerusalem?

    1. (vs 4a)

    2. (vs 4b)

23. What did some of the Pharisees have to say? (vs 5)

24. Read vss 6-13. What happened now? (vs 6)

25a. What did Peter tell the group? (vs 7, briefly)

   b. What was he talking about here? (See 10:1-42, briefly)

   c. What were his main points?
      1. (vs 8b)
      2. (vs 9)
      3. (vs 11)

26. How can our hearts be made clean from sin? (vs 9b)

27. What did Paul and Barnabas talk about? (vs 12)

28a. Read vss 13-21. Who spoke next? (vs 13a)

   b. What was his main point? (vs 19)

   c. What four things did he think they should ask the gentiles to stay away from? (vs 20)

      1.   3.

      2.   4.

29. Read vss 22-29. What was the final decision of the church in Jerusalem?

      1. (vs 22, briefly)

      2. (vs 23a)

30a. What did the letter say about the men who had come to Antioch and told the gentiles they had to be circumcised? (vs 24)

   b. What did the letter ask the gentiles to do? (vs 29)

   c. What did it say about the gentiles being circumcised? (vs 28)

31. Read 30-35. What was the reaction of the Christians in Antioch when they read the letter? (vs 31)

32. What did Judas and Silas do? (vs 32)

33. What did Paul and Barnabas do? (vs 35)

LESSON 13 - THE LETTER TO THE GALATIANS
50 A.D.

Chapter 1 (This letter was written soon after the Jerusalem meeting)

1a. Read vss 1-5. Who wrote this letter? (vs 1a)

b. What does he call himself? (vs 1a)

c. Who was it who sent him out? (vs 1, NIV, Beck)

d. To whom did he address this letter? (vs 2b, locate on your map on page 59, and compare Acts 13:14, 14:1 and 6)

2. Of what great truth does he remind his readers in vs 4a?

3. Read vss 6-10. What was the problem that caused him to write this letter? (vs 6)

4a. What was the cause of this problem? (vs 7b, see also 2:4)

b. What were these men telling the people there? (See 5:2, and compare Acts 15:1)

5. What did Paul say about such men? (vs 9, NIV)

6. Read vss 11-24. What did Paul say about his message?

    1. (vs 11)

    2. (vs 12b)

7a. What was he talking about in vss 13-14? (See Acts 8:3 and 9:1, briefly)

b. What was he talking about in vs 15? (See Acts 9:3-6, briefly)

8. What did he say in vs 17?

Chapter 2

9a. Read vss 1-10. Then reread Acts 15:1-29. How many years after Paul's conversion did this meeting take place? (vs 1a)

b. Where did this meeting take place? (Compare Acts 15:2, 4)

c. What did Paul do there? (vs 2, compare Acts 15:6 and 12)

10. What special point did Paul make about the meeting? (vs 3)

11. What did the apostles and church leaders in Jerusalem do about the Judaizers and their suggestion? (vs 5a)

12a. What did the apostles and leaders do when Paul told them about his teaching? (vs 6b)

  b. What did they have to say about Paul's work and Peter's work?

     1. (vs 7a)

     2. (vs 7b)

13. What title, then, had Jesus given to Paul? (vs 8b, compare Acts 9:15)

14a. Who were the leaders of the church in Jerusalem? (vs 9a)

     1.   2.   3.

  b. What did they do at the conclusion of the meeting? (vs 9a)

15a. What was the final agreement at the end of the meeting? (vs 9b)

  b. What was the only request they made of Paul? (vs 10)

16a. Read vss 11-16. Later on in Antioch what did Peter do when he first arrived? (vs 12a)

  b. What happened when the "men from James" arrived? (vs 12b)

  c. To what group did these men no doubt belong? (See Acts 15:5)

  d. Had they really come from James? (Compare Acts 15:24)

  e. Why did Peter act as he did? (vs 12c)

17. How did Peter's actions affect the rest of the Christians in Antioch?

     1. (vs 13a)

     2. (vs 13b)

18. What did Paul then say to Peter?
     1. (vs 14a)

     2. (vs 14b)

19a. Of what great truth did Paul then remind Peter? (vs 16a)

  b. What had he and Peter both done? (vs 16b)

  c. What did he say about the law as a means of being justified? (vs 16c)

20a. Read vss 17-21. What did Paul say about himself and the Law? (vs 19a)

  b. How and when did this happen? (vs 20a, NIV, RSV)

  c. What was the final result of this?

     1. (vs 20b, last phrase, first sentence, NIV, Beck)

     2. (vs 19b)

Chapter 3

21. Read vss 1-5. What did Paul call the people in Galatia for acting as they did? (vs 1a)

22. What kind of a picture had Paul painted for them? (vs 1b)

23. What three questions did he then ask them?

     1. (vs 2)

     2. (vs 3b)

     3. (vs 4)

24. Read vss 6-9. What did Paul say about Abraham? (vs 6)

25. Who, then, are the true children of Abraham? (vs 7)

26a. According to the Scriptures, how are the gentiles to be justified? (vs 8a)

  b. When did God make this truth clear? (vs 8b)

  c. Where is this promise recorded? (vs 8b, note, NIV, RSV)

27a. Read vss 10-14. What about those people who depend on the Law for salvation? (vs 10a)

  b. What does this mean? (vs 11a)

28a. What has Christ done for us in this respect? (vs 13a, NIV)

  b. How did He do this? (vs 13b)

  c. When did He do this? (vs 13c)

  d. Why did He do this?

      1. (vs 14a)

      2. (vs 14b, Beck)

29. What is thus the main theme of this letter? (vs 11b, Beck, RSV)

30a. Read vss 15-20. What illustration did Paul use here? (vs 15, Beck, RSV)

  b. To what act of God was he comparing the action of this illustration? (vs 16a)

  c. To whom did this promise refer? (vs 16b)

  d. What was the point of the illustration? (vs 17)

31. What, then, is the main thought of this section? (vs 18b)

32a. Why, then, did God give the Law? (vs 19a)

  b. For how long a time was the Law to be in effect? (vs 19b)

33. Read vss 21-29. What purpose did the Law serve during this time? (vs 24, RSV)

34. Now that we are believers, what about our differences of nationality, position, sex, etc?

      1. (vs 28a)

2. (vs 28b)

35a. Since we are all one, to what family do we belong? (vs 29a)

b. What benefit do we enjoy because of this? (vs 29b)

Chapter 4

36a. Read vss 1-7. In the ancient world how was a son treated before he came of age? (vs 2)

b. In a spiritual way how does this illustrate our situation before we become Christians? (vs 3)

37a. What did God do to put an end to our spiritual slavery? (vs 4a)

b. What important prophecy did vs 4b fulfill? (It's in the Book of Genesis)

c. Why was He sent into the world?

1. (vs 5a)

2. (vs 5b)

38. What did God do for us because we are His children? (vs 6a)

39a. Read vss 8-20. What did Paul say about the former condition of the people in Galatia? (vs 8)

b. What question did he ask them? (vs 9b)

c. What were they doing which made him ask this question? (vs 10, compare II Chr. 8:13)

40. How did Paul feel about all his former work among them? (vs 11, Beck, NIV)

41a. Read vss 21-31. In the illustration which covenant did Hagar and Ishmael symbolize? (vs 24b)

b. Which covenant did Sarah and Isaac symbolize? (vs 28)

c. Which one of the two sons did God choose to be His special servant? (vs 30)

d. Which covenant, therefore, should we choose to live under?

Chapter 5

42a. Read vss 1-15. What has Jesus done for us so far as the Law is concerned? (vs 1a)

  b. What must we do, therefore? (vs 1b)

43. What did Paul say about those who let themselves be circumcised? (vs 2)

44a. What word of warning did he give us about our freedom? (vs 13b, TEV)

  b. What does he say we should do? (vs 13c)

45. Read vss 16-26. How did Paul say we Christians must live here on earth?

    1. (vs 16a)

    2. (vs 16b)

46. What are the main fruits of the Spirit? (vs 22-23a)

47. What does Paul say about Christian people? (vs 24)

Chapter 6

48. Read vss 1-10. What general rule does he give us to serve as a guide for our lives?

    1. (vs 8a)

    2. (vs 8b)

49. Read vss 11-18. What is the only thing that makes any real difference to any person? (vs 15b)

LESSON 14 - ACTS 15:36-17:10

Paul Begins His Second Missionary Trip

50-51 A.D.

Chapter 15

1. Read vss 36-41. After some time in Antioch, what was Paul's suggestion to Barnabas? (vs 36)

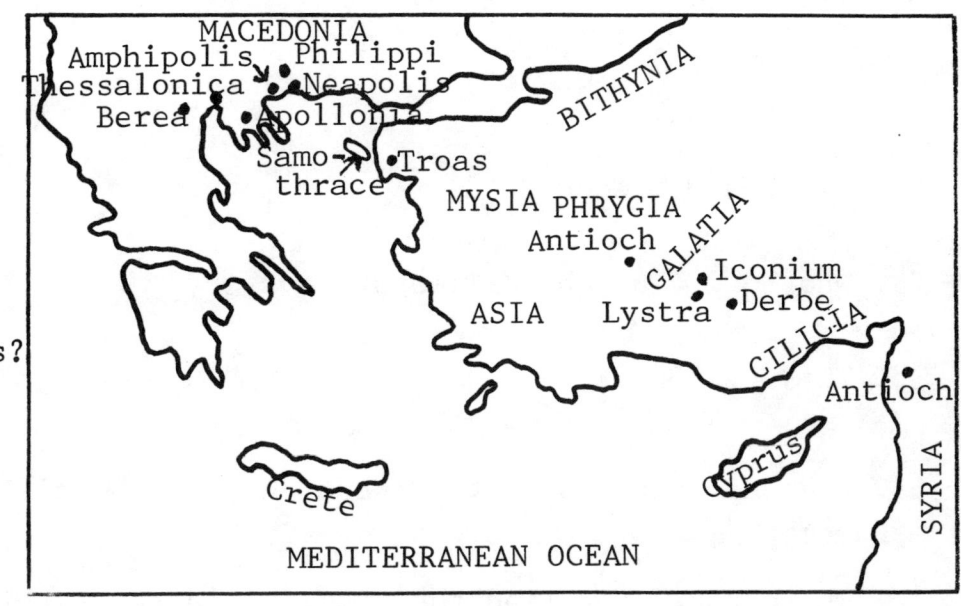

2a. Whom did Barnabas want to take along? (vs 37, see 13:5b)

b. How did Paul feel about this? (vs 38, see 13:13b)

c. What was the result? (vs 39a)

3a. Whom did Barnabas take with him? (vs 39b)

b. Where did he go? (vs 39b, locate on your map)

4a. Whom did Paul choose as his helper? (vs 40a)

b. Where did he go? (vs 41, locate on your map)

c. What did he do there? (vs 41b)

Chapter 16

5. Read vss 1-5. In which two cities did Paul stop first? (vs 1a, locate on your map)

6a. Whom was Paul looking for in Lystra? (vs 1b)

  b. What information does Luke give us about him?

    1. (vs 1c)

    2. (vs 1d)

    3. (vs 2)

    4. (vs 3a, Good News)

7a. What did Paul do to Timothy? (vs 3b)

 b. Why? (vs 3b)

8a. What did they do as they went through the different cities? (vs 4)

 b. Where would you find the original letter setting forth these decisions? (It's in Chapter 15)

9. What was the result of their visits? (vs 5)

    1.

    2.

10a. Read vss 6-10. Through what region did they travel? (vs 6a, locate on your map)

  b. Why? (vs 6b)

11a. Where had they planned to go next? (vs 7a, locate on your map)

  b. How did this plan turn out? (vs 7b)

12. Where did they go then? (vs 8, locate on your map)

13. What happened that night? (vs 9)

14a. What happened the next morning? (vs 10a)

b. Why? (vs 10b)

c. Notice the "we" in vs 10a. What does this tell us? (Compare the pronouns in 7a, 8a, and before)

15a. Read vss 11-15. Where did they go from Troas? (Locate on your map)

    1. (vs 11a)

    2. (vs 11b)

    3. (vs 12a)

b. What information does Luke give us about Philippi? (vs 12b)

    1.

    2.

16a. What did Paul and his friends do on the Sabbath day? (vs 13a)

b. What did they do when they got there? (vs 13b)

17a. What was the name of one of the ladies there? (vs 14a)

b. What else does Luke tell us about her? (vs 14b)

    1.

    2.

    3.

    4.

18a. What happened during the service?

    1. (vs 15a)

    2. (vs 15b)

    3. (vs 15c, last sentence)

19a. Read vss 16-40. Where were Paul and his friends going on this day? (vs 16a)

b. Whom did they meet on the way? (vs 16b)

c. What information does Luke add in vs 16c?

20. What did this girl tell the people about Paul and his friends? (vs 17)

21a. What did Paul finally do? (vs 18b)

   b. What happened? (vs 18c)

22a. What did her owners do? (vs 19)

   b. What accusation did they bring against Paul and Silas? (vss 20-21)

23. What did the Roman governors do?

   1. (vs 22b)

   2. (vs 23b)

24. What did the jailer do to make sure they didn't escape? (vs 24)

   1.

   2.

25. What was going on in the prison that night? (vs 25)

   1.

   2.

26. What happened while this was going on?

   1. (vs 26a)

   2. (vs 26b)

27. What did the jailer do when he woke up? (vs 27b)

28. What did Paul say to him? (vs 28)

29. What did the jailer do then?

    1. (vs 29)

    2. (vs 30)

30. What did Paul answer? (vs 31)

31. What did Paul and Silas do then? (vs 32)

32. What did the jailer do? (vs 33)

    1.

    2.

33. What orders did the governors give the next morning? (vs 35)

34. What message did Paul send back to them?

    1. (vs 37a)

    2. (vs 37b)

35a. What effect did this have on the governors? (vs 38b)

  b. What did they do? (vs 39)

36. What did Paul and Silas do then? (vs 40)

    1.

    2.

    3.

Chapter 17

37. Read vss 1-10. What does the "they" in vs 1 tell us? (Compare question 14c)

38. Where did Paul, Silas and Timothy go now? (vs 1, locate on your map)

    1.   2.   3.

39a. What information does Luke give about Thessalonica? (vs 1b)

  b. What did Paul do?

    1. (vs 2a)

    2. (vs 2b)

40. What were the two main points of Paul's teaching? (vs 3)

    1.

    2.

41. What were the results of his preaching and teaching? (vs 4)

    1.

    2.

42a. What effect did this have on the rest of the Jews? (vs 5a)

  b. What did they do? (vs 5b)

    1.

    2.

43. Where did they go, expecting to find Paul and Silas? (vs 5c)

44. What happened when they didn't find them? (vs 6a)

45a. What accusation did they bring against Paul and Silas? (vs 6b)

  b. What accusation did they bring against the Christians in general?

    1. (vs 7b, Good News)

    2. (vs 7c, Good News)

46. What effect did this have on the people and council? (vs 8)

47. What did the officials finally do? (vs 9)

48. What did the brothers do then? (vs 10)

LESSON 15 - ACTS 17:10-18:5; I THESSALONIANS

Paul Continues His Second Trip and Writes to the Thessalonians

51 A.D.

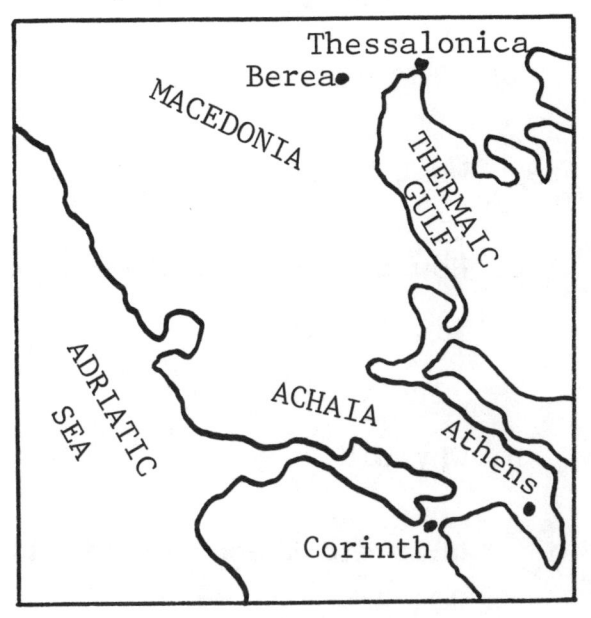

Chapter 17

1a. Read vss 10-14. Where was Paul now? (vs 10a)

 b. What did he do as soon as he arrived? (vs 10b)

2a. What does Luke say about the Jews in Berea? (vs 11a)

 b. How did they receive Paul's message? (vs 11b)

   1.

   2.

3. What was the result of Paul's work there? (vs 12)

   1.

   2.

4a. What happened after Paul had been there a short while? (vs 13a)

 b. What did they do? (vs 13b)

5a. What did the brothers in Berea do then? (vs 14a)

 b. What did Silas and Timothy do? (vs 14b)

6a. Read vss 15-21. Where did Paul go now? (vs 15a, locate on your map)

 b. What message did Paul send back with the men from Berea? (vs 15b)

7a. How did Paul feel while he was waiting for his friends to join him? (vs 16, Good News)

b. Why? (vs 16)

8. What did he do while he was waiting?

    1. (vs 17a, Good News, Beck)

    2. (vs 17b)

9. What happened one day in the town square? (vs 18a)

10a. How did these men receive Paul's message?

    1. (vs 18b)

    2. (vs 18c)

  b. Why did they say this? (vs 18d)

11. What did these men finally do? (vs 19a, Good News, Beck)

12. What did the members of the Court say to Paul?

    1. (vs 19b)

    2. (vs 20)

13. What information did Luke add in vs 21?

14a. Read vss 22-34. How did Paul start his speech to the Court? (vs 22b)

  b. Why did he say this? (vs 23a)

15. What did Paul say he was going to do? (vs 23b, Good News, NIV)

16a. What was the first thing Paul told them about God? (vs 24a)

  b. What else did he tell them? (vs 24b, Good News, Beck, RSV)

17a. What was the next thing he told them about God? (vs 25a, Good News)

  b. Why? (vs 25b)

18. Where did all the nations of the world come from? (vs 26a)

19. When God created man what did He hope man would do? (vs 27a)

20a. Why should it be easy to find Him?

    1. (vs 27b)

    2. (vs 28a)

21. What was the main point of these last five verses? (vs 29)

22a. What did Paul say about man's history up to the time of Christ's birth? (vs 30a)

  b. But what was God telling people now? (vs 30b)

  c. Why? (vs 31a)

23. What has God done to prove that all this is true? (vs 31b)

24. What happened when Paul said that God has raised Jesus back to life from the dead?

    1. (vs 32a)

    2. (vs 32b)

25a. What was the result of this speech to the Council? (vs 34a)

  b. What was the name of one of these? (vs 34b)

26. What were the results among the other people who were listening? (vs 34c)

Chapter 18:1-5

27. Where did Paul go next? (vs 1, locate on your map)

28a. Whom did he meet there? (vs 2a)

  b. What information does Luke give us about this man? (vs 2b)

    1.

78

       2.

29a. What did Paul do after he visited this couple in their home? (vs 3)

    1.

    2.

  b. Why? (vs 3)

30. What did Paul do every Sabbath day? (vs 4, Good News)

31a. What happened after a few weeks? (vs 5a)

  b. What did Paul do now? (vs 5b)

I Thessalonians (This letter was written at this time)

Introduction

32a. Read Acts 17:1-10, remembering that after this Paul had visited briefly in Berea, Athens and Corinth. What had happened when Paul left Berea? (Acts 17:14b)

  b. What had happened after this? (I Thess. 2:17-18a, esp. 18a)

  c. Why hadn't he been able to come? (vs 18b)

  d. What did Paul mean by this? (See Acts 17:13-14, briefly)

33a. What had Paul done, therefore? (I Thess. 3:1-2)

  b. What was Timothy to do there? (vss 2b-3a)

    1.

    2.

  c. What kind of trials (NIV) troubles (Beck) afflictions (RSV) was Paul worried about? (vs 3a, compare Acts 17:5-7 with I Thess. 2:14)

34. Why did Paul write this letter to them at this time?

    1. (vs 3:6a)

    2. (vs 3:6b)

Chapter 1

35a. Who wrote this letter? (vs 1a)

b. To whom was it addressed? (vs 1b)

36a. Read vss 2-10. What were the things about the Christians in Thessalonica that made a lasting impression on Paul? (vs 3)

    1.

    2.

    3.

b. What was the work and labor that Paul was writing about? (vs 8a, Beck, RSV)

Chapter 2

37. Read vss 1-16. How had the people in Thessalonica received Paul's message? (vs 13)

38a. What comparison did Paul make between the Christians in Thessalonica and those in Judea? (vs 14b)

b. Who else had the Jews attacked and killed? (vs 15)

39. Read vss 19-20. What did Paul call the Christians in Thessalonica? (vs 20)

Chapter 3

40. Read vss 6-13. What had Timothy's good report about the Thessalonians done for Paul? (vs 7)

41. What was Paul praying for and hoping for now? (vss 10-11, briefly)

Chapter 4

42. Read vss 1-8. What is God's will for all Christians? (vs 3a, compare vs 7)

43a. Read vss 9-12. What practical rules does Paul give us in this respect? (vs 11)

    1.

2.

3.

   b. What will such a life do for us? (vs 12)

      1.

      2.

44a. Read vss 13-18. What was one of the problems of the Christians in Thessalonica? (vs 13, compare 15b)

   b. Of what fact did Paul remind them here? (vs 14a)

   c. What assurance does this give us Christians? (vs 14b)

45. How does Paul describe Christ's return? (vs 16a-c, NIV, RSV)

    1.

    2.

    3.

46. What will happen when He returns?

    1. (vs 16d)

    2. (vs 17a)

    3. (vs 17b)

Chapter 5

47. Read vss 1-11. What does Paul say about the Day of Jesus' return? (vs 2, compare Matt. 24:42-43)

48a. What advantage do we have as Christians? (vs 4)

   b. What good advice does Paul give us about Jesus' return? (vs 6)

      1.

      2.

49. What, therefore, did Christ accomplish by His death? (vs 10)

LESSON 16 - II THESSALONIANS, ACTS 18:5-22

Paul Writes Again to the Thessalonians, Finishes His Work in Corinth and Returns Home

51-53 A.D.

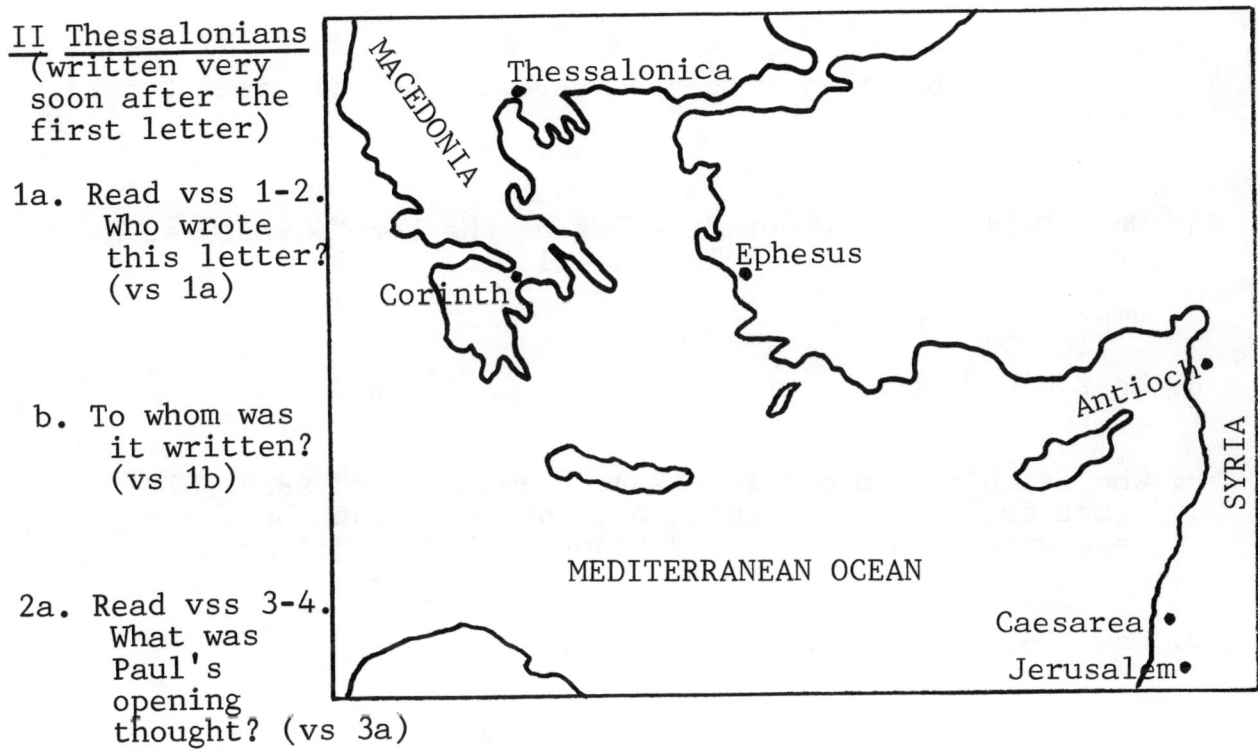

II Thessalonians
(written very soon after the first letter)

1a. Read vss 1-2. Who wrote this letter? (vs 1a)

b. To whom was it written? (vs 1b)

2a. Read vss 3-4. What was Paul's opening thought? (vs 3a)

b. Why? (vs 3b)

   1.

   2.

3. What else did he tell them? (vs 4)

4a. Read vss 5-12. What is God's purpose in permitting Christians to suffer? (vs 5b, RSV, Beck)

b. When will all our sufferings come to an end? (vs 7b)

5a. What about those who are unbelievers? (vs 8)

b. What is meant by eternal death or destruction? (vs 9b)

Chapter 2

6. Read vss 1-12. What was Paul writing about in this paragraph? (vs 1)

    1.

    2.

7. What had apparently happened there in Thessalonica? (vs 2, Beck)

8a. When Paul writes about "the Day of the Lord", what was he talking about? (See I Thess. 4:15-16)

   The day when...

 b. What did Paul say here about that Day? (vs 3)

 c. Who is this "man of sin" (KJ), "lawlessness" (RSV, NIV) (better "son of Destruction", the awful man who destroys everything, Matt. 24:15)? (Compare I John 2:18a)

 d. How does Paul describe him here? (vs 4)

    1.

    2.

9a. What did they already know about this Antichrist?

    1. (vs 6a)

    2. (vs 6b, compare 3b)

 b. What does Paul say about his lawlessness?

    1. (vs 7a)

    2. (vs 7b)

10. What will happen when he is unmasked? (vs 8, Beck, RSV)

11a. Who is behind the appearance and work of this wicked man? (vs 9)

  b. What kind of "tools" does he use?

     1. (vs 9b)

     2. (vs 10a, RSV)

12. What effects do these things have on the people of the world?

     1. (vs 10b, NIV)

     2. (vs 11)

13. What, then, will be the final result on Judgment Day? (vs 12)

14a. Read vss 13-17. What must we always remember as Christians? (vs 13a)

  b. What had to be done to us to make this possible? (vs 13b, Beck)

  c. Who has done this for us? (vs 13b)

  d. How did He do this? (vs 13, last phrase)

15a. What did this original choice of God lead Him to do? (vs 14a)

  b. Why? (vs 14b)

16. What was Paul asking them to do, therefore? (vs 15)

17. What has God done for us by saving us from sin and death? (vs 16b)

Chapter 3

18a. Read vss 1-2. What did Paul ask the Thessalonians to do for him? (vs 1a)

b. Why? (vs 1b)

c. What else did he ask them to pray for? (vs 2)

19. Read vss 3-5. What was Paul's prayer for the Thessalonians? (vs 5, Beck)

20a. Read vss 6-18. What were Paul's instructions in vs 6?

b. What general rule did he lay down? (vs 10b)

21. What good advice did he give the Christians in Thessalonica? (vs 13, NIV, Beck)

22a. What did Paul say they should do to those who refused to follow his orders? (vs 14a)

b. Why? (vs 14b)

Acts, Chapter 18

23a. Read vss 5-6. What was Paul doing there in Corinth during this time? (vs 5b)

b. What was he trying to do? (vs 5c, Good News)

24a. What happened after a short while? (vs 6a)

b. What did Paul do then? (vs 6b)

c. What did he say to them? (vs 6c)

    1.

    2.

    3.

25a. Read vss 7-11. Where did Paul go now to hold his Bible classes and services? (vs 7a)

b. Where was this house located? (vs 7b, Good News, Beck)

26. Who were the other people who joined Paul as members of his new congregation? (vs 8a)

    1.

    2.

27. How does Luke describe the results of Paul's work in Corinth? (vs 8b, Good News)

28a. What did the Lord do to strengthen and encourage Paul? (vs 9a)

  b. What did He say to Paul? (vs 9b)

    1.

    2.

    3.

29a. How long did Paul stay there in Corinth? (vs 11a)

  b. What was he doing all this time? (vs 11b)

30a. Read vss 12-17. What happened during this time? (vs 12)

    1.

    2.

  b. When did this happen? (vs 12a, see note in the Good News)

  c. What did they accuse Paul of doing? (vs 13, Good News)

31a. What did Gallio answer?

    1. (vs 14)

    2. (vs 15a)

    3. (vs 15b)

b. Then what did he do? (vs 16, Good News, Beck)

32a. What did the citizens of Corinth do then? (vs 17a)

   b. What did Gallio do about this? (vs 17b)

33a. Read vss 18-22. What did Paul do after this incident? (vs 18a)

   b. Then what did he do? (vs 18a)

   c. Who else went with him? (vs 18b)

34a. What did Paul do before he left Cenchrea? (vs 18c)

   b. Why? (vs 18d)

35a. Where did Paul go first? (vs 19a, locate on your map)

   b. What did he do there? (vs 19b)

   c. What did Priscilla and Aquila do? (vs 19a)

36a. What did Paul do when the people there asked him to stay? (vs 20)

   b. What did he say? (vs 21a)

37a. Where did Paul go now? (vs 22a, locate on your map)

   b. What did he do next? (vs 22b, Good News, locate on your map)

38. Then where did he go? (vs 22c, locate on your map)

LESSON 17 - ACTS 18:23-19:22; I CORINTHIANS 1-5

Paul Begins His Third Trip, Goes to Ephesus, and Writes a Letter to the Christians in Corinth

53-55 A.D.

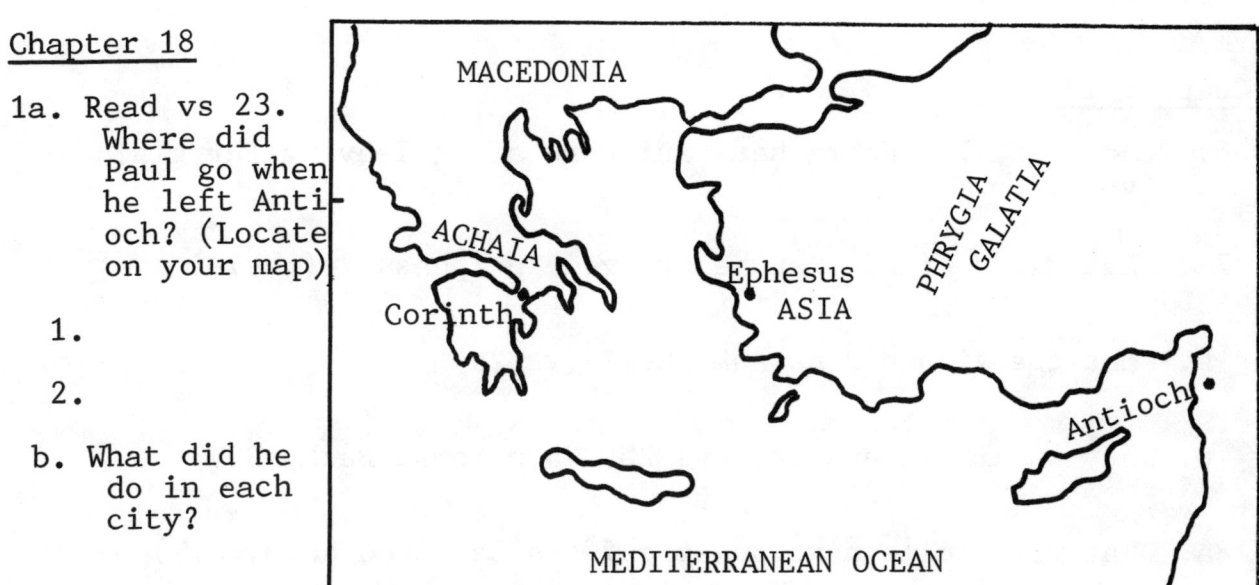

Chapter 18

1a. Read vs 23. Where did Paul go when he left Antioch? (Locate on your map)

   1.

   2.

b. What did he do in each city?

c. To what city was he going on this trip? (vs 19:1)

2a. Read vss 24-28. Who had come to Ephesus since Paul was there the first time? (vs 24a)

b. What information does Luke give about this man?

   1. (vs 24)

   2. (vs 24)

   3. (vs 24)

   4. (vs 24)

   5. (vs 25a)

   6. (vs 25b)

   7. (vs 25c)

3a. What did this man do when he came to Ephesus? (vs 26a)

b. What did Priscilla and Aquila do? (vs 26b)

4a. What did Apollos wish to do after this? (vs 27a, locate on map)

b. What did the brothers in Ephesus do? (vs 27b)

5a. What did Apollos do when he arrived in Athens and Corinth? (vs 27c)

  b. Why? (vs 28)

Chapter 19

6. Read vss 1-7. Where had Paul gone after leaving Phrygia? (vs 1, Good News, NIV)

7a. What did he find when he arrived in Ephesus? (vs 1b)

  b. What question did he ask them? (vs 2a)

  c. What was their answer? (vs 2b, Good News, Beck, RSV)

8a. What was Paul's next question? (vs 3a, Good News, NIV)

  b. What did they reply? (vs 3b)

9a. What did Paul say about John's baptism? (vs 4a)

  b. What was John's main message? (vs 4b)

10a. What happened then? (vs 5)

  b. What happened when Paul put his hands on them? (vs 6)

  c. How many men were there in this group? (vs 7)

11a. Read vss 8-12. Where did Paul go now? (vs 8a)

  b. What did he do there?

    1. (vs 8a, Good News)

    2. (vs 8b, Good News, Beck)

12. What happened at the end of the three months? (vs 9a)

   1.

   2.

   3.

13a. What did Paul do then? (vs 9b)

  b. Where did he go? (vs 9c)

  c. What did he do there? (vs 9c)

  d. How long did he keep on doing this? (vs 10a)

14. What were the results of this work? (vs 10b)

15a. What did the Lord do to help Paul? (vs 11)

  b. What example does Luke give us in vs 12?

16a. Read vss 13-17. Who was this incident about? (vs 14)

  b. What were they doing? (vs 13a)

17. What did they do when they heard about Paul? (vs 13b)

18a. What happened one day when two of them were doing this? (vs 15)

  b. What did the spirit do then? (vs 15)

   1.

   2.

19. What effect did this have on the people at Ephesus? (vs 17)

   1.

   2.

20a. Read vss 18-20. What happened after this?

   1. (vs 18)

   2. (vs 19a)

 b. What was the value of the books? (vs 19b. A drachma was a day's wages, worth about $50.00 today)

21. What do these last two verses show us? (vs 20)

22a. Read vss 21-22. What did Paul decide to do now? (vs 21a)

 b. What were his plans after he got to Jerusalem? (vs 21b)

 c. What did Paul do first? (vs 22a)

 d. What did he do after this? (vs 22b)

I Corinthians (This letter was written at this time)

Chapter 1

23a. Read vss 1-3. Who wrote this letter? (vs 1a)

 b. Who was Sosthenes? (See Acts 18:17, Good News)

 c. What did Paul call the Christians in Corinth? (vs 2a, KJ, RSV)

24. Read vss 4-9. As Paul thought about the people in Corinth, why was he so thankful?

   1. (vs 5, Beck)

   2. (vs 7a, Beck)

25a. What is our comfort as Christians as we face the devil and all our troubles? (vs 8a)

 b. What is our hope as Christians? (vs 8b)

26a. Read vss 10-17. What was one of the problems there in Corinth? (vss 10-11)

b. What did Paul suggest as the cure? (vs 10a and c)

27. Read vss 18-31. What did Paul say about the message of the cross?
    1. (vs 18a)
    2. (vs 18b)

28a. What is it that is really foolishness? (vs 20b)

b. Why? (vs 21a)

29a. How then, can people come to know God and be saved? (vs 21b)

b. What does this mean to all of us who are believers? (vs 29)

c. Why? (vs 30a)

30. What four things has Christ given us? (vs 30b)
    1.
    2.
    3.
    4.

Chapter 2

31. Read vss 1-5. How did Paul summarize his message? (vs 2b)

32a. Read vss 6-16. How else did he describe his work? (vs 7a, NIV, Beck)

b. When did God lay out His plan of salvation? (vs 7b)

c. How has God revealed all this to men? (vs 10a)

Chapter 3

33. Read vss 1-4. What did Paul say was the reason for their quarrels and divisions? (vss 1b and 3a, RSV, Beck)

34a. Read vss 5-9a. How did Paul describe his work in Corinth? (vs 6a)

  b. How did he describe Apollos' work there? (vs 6a)

  c. Who, however, was the one who made the work succeed? (vs 6b)

35a. Read vss 9b-23. What does Paul call the church in Corinth? (vs 9b, last two words, compare vs 16a)

  b. What was Paul's work? (vs 10a)

  c. What work did Apollos and the others who came later do? (vs 10b)

  d. What word of caution did Paul give to the later workers?

    1. (vs 10c)

    2. (vs 11a, to "laid")

  e. And what is the foundation of the Church and every Christian congregation? (vs 11b)

Chapter 4

36a. Read vss 1-7. What does Paul call himself and Apollos? (vs 1a)

  b. What position had Christ given them? (vs 1b, Beck)

  c. What is the one quality above all others that a master looks for in a man he appoints to manage his business? (vs 2, Beck, RSV)

37. Read vss 8-13. How does Paul describe his life as an apostle? (Sum up briefly vss 11-13)

38. Read vss 14-21. What was Paul asking the people in Corinth to do here? (vs 16)

Chapter 5

39a. Read vss 1-13. What problem was Paul writing about here? (vs 1b)

  b. What does Paul say the congregation must do? (vss 2b and 3b)

  c. What general rule does this illustrate? (vs 9, RSV)

LESSON 18 - I CORINTHIANS 6-15
55 A.D.

Chapter 6

1a. Read vss 1-8. What was the problem Paul was writing about here? (vss 1 and 6)

 b. What two suggestions did Paul make as possible solutions?

   1. (vs 5)

   2. (vs 7b)

2a. Read vss 9-11. What important principle is given here about getting into the Kingdom of Heaven? (vs 9a, compare Rev. 21:27, RSV, Beck, NIV)

 b. How is it possible for us to get into the Kingdom? (vs 11b)

3a. Read vss 12-20. What is one rule that a Christian may follow because Christ has set us free from the Law? (vs 12a and c, first phrase in each)

 b. What two things, however, must a Christian also remember?

   1. (vs 12b)

   2. (vs 12d, RSV, Beck)

 c. What, then, are the best things to remember?

   1. (vs 15a)

   2. (vs 19a)

   3. (vs 20)

Chapter 7

4a. Read vss 1-16. What subject is Paul writing about here? (vss 2 and 8-9, see chapter title in NIV)

 b. What general rule is given in vs 3?

 c. What rule is given in vss 10b and 11b?

5. Read vss 17-40. Why did Paul think that it was better to remain single?

   1. (vss 32 and 34b, combine) The single person...

2. (vss 33 and 34c, combine) The married person...

3. (vs 35b)

Chapter 8

6. Read vss 1-13. What problem was Paul writing about here? (vs 1a, RSV)

7a. Of what truth does Paul remind us in vs 2? (Beck, RSV)

  b. What is the only really essential kind of knowledge? (vs 3b, compare 1:18-25, esp. vs 25, and 2:6-7)

8a. What does Paul have to say about idols in general? (vs 4a)

  b. Of what all-important truth does Paul remind us in vs 4b?

  c. What about food offered to an idol, then?

     1. (vs 8a)

     2. (vs 8b)

9. What, then, would be the danger of eating food that had been sacrificed to some idol? (vss 11a and 13)

Chapter 9

10. Read vss 1-11a. What did Paul say about his right as an apostle? (vss 4 and 11)

11a. Read vss 11b-18. What did he say about using his right? (vss 12b and 15a)

  b. Why was Paul working to spread the Good News? (vs 17b, NIV, RSV)

12. Read vss 19-23. What was his other motive? (vs 23)

13a. Read vss 24-27. What does Paul say about the athletes who took part in the Olympic games? (vs 25a, NIV, Beck)

  b. What sort of a crown (award) did they receive? (vs 25b, NIV)

  c. What sort of a crown (award) are we going to receive if we win in our contest? (vs 25c, see II Tim. 4:8, James 1:12, I Pet. 5:4, Rev. 2:10 and 3:11)

  d. Why was Paul so careful about the way he lived? (vs 27b, Beck)

Chapter 10

14a. Read vss 1-13. What series of events was Paul talking about here? (vs 1-10, briefly)

  b. Of what was the fact that they were with Moses in the cloud and water a type or symbol? (vs 2, compare Gal. 3:27)

  c. Of what was the fact that they ate and drank spiritual food a type or symbol? (vss 3-4, compare vs 16)

  d. Why wasn't God pleased with the Israelites? (vss 5-10, briefly)

  e. Why did God record all these things? (vs 11)

15. What does Paul say about the tests, or troubles which God sends upon us? (vs 13)

    1.

    2.

16a. Read vss 14-22. What are we doing when we drink the wine from the cup at the communion table? (vs 16a, Beck)

  b. What are we doing when we eat the bread? (vs 16b, Beck)

  c. What do we learn from the fact that there was <u>one</u> loaf of bread at the first Lord's supper? (vs 17a)

  d. Of what was Paul warning the early Christians about in this section? (vss 19-21, briefly, esp. vs 21)

17. Read vss 23-11:1, and compare with 8:1-13. What should be our aim in all our actions?

    1. (vss 24 and 33b)

    2. (vs 32)

Chapter 11

18a. Read vss 2-16. What three basic truths are given here?

    1. (vs 3a)

    2. (vs 3b)

    3. (vs 3c)

b. What two general principles did Paul give the early Christians?

   1. (vs 7a)

   2. (vs 10, Beck, RSV)

c. What other principle must also be kept in mind? (vs 11)

19. Read vss 17-22 and compare with 1:10-11. What did Paul scold the Corinthian Christians for here?

    1. (vs 18a)

    2. (vs 21)

20. Read vss 23-34. What two warnings does Paul give us regarding our use of the Lord's Supper?

    1. (vs 27)

    2. (vs 29, Beck)

Chapter 12

21a. Read vss 1-11. What is the subject of chapters 12-14? (vs 1, Beck)

  b. Of what did Paul remind the Corinthian Christians? (vs 2)

  c. What two general statements did he make about the Holy Spirit?

     1. (vs 3a)

     2. (vs 3b)

22. What three general statements did he make about spiritual gifts? (NIV, RSV)

    1. (vs 4)

    2. (vs 5)

    3. (vs 6)

23. What rule does the Holy Spirit follow in passing out His gifts? (vs 7, Beck)

24. What are some of the Spirit's gifts that Paul lists here?

    1. (vs 8a)

    2. (vs 8b)

3. (vs 9a)

4. (vs 9b)

5. (vs 10a)

6. (vs 10b)

7. (vs 10c)

8. (vs 10d)

9. (vs 10e)

25a. Read vss 12-31. What does Paul use as the illustration in this section? (vss 12a and 27))

b. What is the main point of the illustration? (vs 12a)

c. What is the point of vss 14-20? (In one short sentence, see vs 17 especially, compare vss 8-10)

d. What is necessary if the body is to be and remain healthy? (vs 25, your own words)

e. How does Paul apply all this to us? (vs 27)

Chapter 13

26a. Read vss 1-13. What is the greatest of all the Spirit's gifts? (vss 1-3 and 13)

b. Why?
1. (vs 5b, see also 10:24 and 33b)

2. (vs 8a, Beck, RSV)

Chapter 14

27a. Read vss 1-5. What is the next greatest gift? (vs 1b)

b. Why (vs 4b)

28a. Read vss 6-25. What does Paul say about speaking in tongues (other languages) in the church service? (vss 9b and 16b)

b. What does Paul say about this gift? (vs 19)

29. Read vss 26-40. What general rule does Paul lay down about the use of our gifts? (vs 26c)

Chapter 15

30. Read vss 1-11. How does Paul sum up the Gospel?

    1. (vs 3b)

    2. (vs 4a)

    3. (vs 4b)

31. How many occasions does Paul list on which Jesus appeared to His followers after His resurrection? (vss 5-8, count them)

32. What did Paul say about himself?

    1. (vs 9)

    2. (vs 10a)

33a. Read vss 12-20. What was another problem in Corinth? (vs 12b)

  b. What was Paul's answer to this problem?

    1. (vs 13)

    2. (vs 17)

    3. (vs 20)

34. Read vss 21-34. What two great facts must we remember?

    1. (vs 22a)

    2. (vs 22b)

35. Read vss 35-58. What does Paul say about our resurrection bodies?

    1. (vs 42b)   4. (vs 44b)

    2. (vs 43b)   5. (vs 49b)

    3. (vs 43d)

36a. What was the "secret" Paul revealed in vs 51b?

  b. When will this happen? (vs 52a, see Matt. 24:31, I Th. 4:16)

  c. Why is this change necessary?

    1. (vs 53a, Beck) Because our bodies are

    2. (vs 53b, Beck) Because our bodies are

LESSON 19 - I CORINTHIANS 16; ACTS 19:23-20:1a; II CORINTHIANS 10-13

A Riot Occurs in Ephesus and Paul Writes a Second Letter to Corinth

56 A.D.

I Corinthians 16

1a. Read vss 1-4. What were all of Paul's congregations doing at this time? (vs 1a)

 b. What instructions did Paul give the Christians in Corinth?

    1. (vs 2, NIV, RSV)

    2. (vs 3)

2. Read vss 5-12. What were Paul's plans for the immediate future?

    1. (vs 8)

    2. (vs 5)

    3. (vs 6)

Acts 19

3a. Read vss 23-27. Where was Paul now? (See vs 1)

 b. What happened at this time? (vs 23)

 c. Who started the riot? (vs 24a)

 d. What was he manufacturing? (vs 24b)

 e. What does vs 24 tell us about his business?

4a. What did this man do at this time? (vs 25a, NIV)

 b. Of what did he remind them? (vs 25b)

5a. Why was Demetrius so upset? (vs 26a, NIV, Beck, 26b Good News)

b. What had Paul been telling the people? (vs 26b)

c. What was Demetrius afraid of?

    1. (vs 27a, Beck)

    2. (vs 27b)

    3. (vs 27c)

6. Read vss 28-31. What did the rest of the workers do when they heard this? (vs 28a)

7. What was the result of their shouting? (vs 29a)

8. What happened now? (vs 29b)

9a. What did Paul want to do? (vs 30a)

 b. Who stopped him from doing so? (vs 30b)

 c. What did some of the city officials do? (vs 31)

10a. Read vss 32-41. What was going on inside the theater? (vs 32a)

 b. What about the people who had gathered there? (vs 32b)

11a. Whom did the Jews bring in as their spokesman? (vs 33a)

 b. What was he going to do? (vs 33b)

12. What was the reaction of the crowd? (vs 34)

13a. Who took charge of the crowd now? (vs 35a)

 b. What did he do? (vs 35a)

 c. Then what did he tell the people to do? (vs 36b)

 d. What did he say about Gaius and Aristarchus? (vs 37, NIV, Beck)

 e. What did he say about Demetrius and his friends? (vs 38)

f. What else did he tell the people? (vs 40a)

g. What did he do then? (vs 41)

14. Read 20:1a. What did Paul do now? (as far as "them", Beck, NIV)

II Corinthians 10-13 (These 4 chapters were a separate letter which Paul wrote at this time. The first 9 chapters were written a short time later).

Chapter 10

15a. Read vss 1-6. What was Paul doing as he begins this letter? (vs 1a, NIV, Beck)

b. Why was he doing this? (vs 2a, NIV, Beck)

c. What problem caused Paul to write this letter? (vs 2b, beginning "some people", NIV; "some men", Beck)

d. What were Paul's plans? (vs 2a, "when I come" NIV, compare Acts 19:21a)

16a. What was Paul's answer to these accusations? (vs 3)

b. What kind of weapons was Paul using to fight with? (vs 4, see Ephesians 6:17b)

c. What did he say about these weapons?

    1. (vs 4b)

    2. (vs 5a)

17. What else did Paul do as a good soldier of Christ's? (vs 5b)

18. What did he tell the Christians in Corinth? (vs 6)

19a. Read vss 7-17. What does vs 7b tell us about what was going on in Corinth at this time?

b. What fact was Paul emphasizing in vs 8a?

c. Why had Jesus given him this authority? (vs 8b)

20a. What were their new preachers saying about Paul? (vs 10, RSV)

b. What was Paul's answer to them? (vs 11, NIV)

21a. What did Paul intend to do? (vs 13, NIV)

   1. (vs 13a)

   2. (vs 13b)

  b. Of what fact did Paul remind the people?

   1. (vs 14a, NIV)

   2. (vs 14b, RSV, Beck)

  c. What was Paul's hope in bringing the Gospel to Corinth? (vs 15b-16a, RSV, NIV)

  d. What little "dig" did Paul add for the benefit of the new preachers? (vs 16b, NIV)

  e. Of what truth did Paul remind everyone? (vs 18, Beck)

Chapters 11-12

22a. Read 11:1-15. What was Paul's request of the Christians in Corinth? (11:1, NIV, Beck)

  b. Of what did he remind them?

   1. (vs 2a)

   2. (vs 2b)

  c. What was Paul afraid of? (vs 3b)

23a. What did Paul say these new preachers were doing? (vs 4)

   1.

   2.

   3.

  b. What does he call these men? (vs 5, NIV, Beck)

c. What does Paul say about himself?

   1. (vs 5)

   2. (vs 6)

24a. What does Paul say about his work in Corinth?

   1. (vs 7)

   2. (vs 8)

b. Who had supplied Paul's needs while he was working in Corinth? (vs 9b)

25a. What does Paul call the new super apostles in vs 13?

   1. (vs 13a)

   2. (vs 13b)

b. For whom were they working? (vss 14-15)

26a. Read 11:16-29. What does Paul say he was going to do now? (vss 16b, and 18)

b. What does he suggest the false apostles have done in vs 20?

   1.

   2.

   3.

   4.

   5.

c. What does Paul say about himself? (vs 21a)

27. What does Paul present as his credentials as a genuine apostle? (vss 23-27, briefly)

28. Read 11:30-12:10. What did Paul brag about here?

   1. (12:1)

   2. (vss 11:30 and 12:9b)

29a. What did Jesus tell Paul when Paul asked Him to remove his physical affliction? (12:9)

   1.

   2.

 b. What does this mean for us Christians? (vs 10b)

30a. Read 12:11-21. What did Paul say to the Christians in Corinth in vs 11b? (Beck, 2nd sentence)

 b. Why? (vs 12)

31a. What did Paul say about his immediate plans? (vs 14a)

 b. What did Paul say he wanted from the Christians in Corinth? (vs 14b)

 c. What did Paul say about himself in vs 15a?

 d. What did he say about everything he had done and was still doing? (vs 19b, beginning "everything...")

32. What was Paul afraid of regarding his coming visit?

   1. (vs 20a)

   2. (vs 21b)

   3. (vs 21c)

Chapter 13

33a. Read vss 1-13. What did Paul tell his readers in vs 2b?

 b. What did he tell them to do in vs 5a?

34. What did Paul say he was praying for?

   1. (vs 7a)

   2. (vs 9b)

LESSON 20 - ACTS 20:1-2; II CORINTHIANS 1-9

Paul Goes to Macedonia and Writes a Third Letter to Corinth

Fall, 56 A.D.

Acts 20

1a. Read vss 1-2. Where was Paul now? (vs 1, compare 19:35)

b. Where did he go when he finished his second letter? (vs 1b, locate on map on page 87)

c. What did he do? (vs 2a)

II Corinthians 1-9 (Written from Macedonia at this time)

Chapters 1-2:4

2a. Read 1:1-2. Who wrote this letter? (vs 1a)

b. To whom was the letter addressed? (vs 1b)

3a. Read 1:3-11. What does Paul say about God in vs 4a?

b. Why? (vs 4b)

c. What kind of sufferings was Paul thinking about here? (vs 5a)

4a. What does Paul say about his own sufferings and troubles in Asia? (vs 9a)

b. What had Paul learned from this? (vs 9b)

5. How did Paul say his friends in Corinth could help him? (vs 11a)

6. Read vss 1:12-2:4. What was Paul's hope so far as the Christians in Corinth were concerned? (vs 14b)

7a. What were Paul's enemies (see Lesson 19, question 15c) saying about him because he had changed his plans? (vs 17b, NIV)

b. What was Paul's explanation for his change of plans? (vs 23b and 2:4a, Beck)

8. What is the special seal or mark that God puts on all those who belong to Him? (vss 22b)

105

9a. What did Paul say about his feelings as he wrote the last letter (II Cor. 10-13)? (vs 2:4a)

   b. What did he say his main purpose in writing was? (vs 2:4b)

Chapter 2

10a. Read vss 5-11. What problem was Paul writing about here? (See I Cor. 5:1)

   b. What had the people in the congregation done about it? (vs 6a, see I Cor. 5:2b)

11a. What did Paul say they should do now? (vs 7a)

   b. What does this indicate about the man? (vs 7b, see Luke 17:3b)

   c. What would this suggested action show the man? (vs 8)

12a. Read vss 12-17. Why hadn't Paul stayed on in Troas to work? (vs 13a)

   b. What did Paul say God was accomplishing through his work? (vs 14b)

   c. How did he say the unbelievers felt about him? (vs 16a)

   d. How did he say the believers felt about him? (vs 16b)

Chapter 3

13. Read vss 1-6. What does Paul call the Corinthians in vs 2?

14. What is the basis of our confidence as Christians regarding our ability to do things? (vs 5, Beck, RSV)

15. What did Paul say about himself and us in vs 6a? (Beck, NIV)

16a. What did he say about the covenant under which we live? (vs 6b, NIV)

   1. It isn't...

   2. but...

   b. What is the great difference between these two covenants? (vs 6c)

17a. Read vss 7-11. What is the written covenant of which Paul was speaking here? (vs 7, compare Ex. 31:18)

   b. What did he say about God's glory which accompanied the giving of this covenant? (vs 7b, see Ex. 34:35)

c. What comparison did he make in vss 9 and 11?

18a. Read vss 12-18. What did Paul say about the people of Israel in Moses' time? (vs 14a)

b. What did he say about the Jews in his day? (vs 14b and 15)

c. Who is the only one who can remove this veil? (vs 14c)

d. When does it become possible for a person to understand God's Word? (vs 16)

19a. What does Paul say about the Spirit in vs 17b?

b. What kind of a change is taking place in us Christians? (vs 18)

c. How is this change being effected? (vs 18a, RSV)

Chapters 4-5:10

20a. Read vss 1-6. Who would the god of this world be? (vs 4a, compare I John 5:19)

b. What has he done? (vs 4, NIV, RSV)

21. What has the Holy Spirit done for us in this respect? (vs 6)

22a. Read vss 7-15. Of what two truths does Paul remind us in vs 10?

   1.

   2.

b. What was it that brought about the death of Jesus? (I Cor. 15:3)

23. Of what else does Paul remind us as Christians in vs 11a?

24. What is it, then, that causes us to speak about Jesus to others? (vs 13a)

25. Read 4:16-5:10. How does Paul sum up our present situation? (vs 16b)

26. What else does he say to encourage us? (vs 17)

27a. How do we cope with all our problems in this world? (vs 18a)

　b. Why? (vs 18b)

28a. What does Paul call our body in 5:1a?

　b. What does he say will happen when this tent is taken down? (vs 5:1b)

　c. What is our real situation, then, as Christians in this world? (vs 5:6b)

　d. How do we feel about this? (vs 5:8b)

　e. What is our one great aim as Christians? (vs 5:9)

29. Of what other fact does Paul remind us in vs 5:10?

Chapters 5:11-6:2

30a. Read vss 11-15. What is it that controls our lives and all our actions as Christians? (vs 14a)

　b. On what fact is our love for Christ based? (vs 14b)

　c. What was His purpose in doing this? (vs 15)

31. Read vss 16-6:2. How does Paul describe our new situation as Christians? (vs 17)

　　1.

　　2.

　　3.

32a. Who has brought this change about? (vs 18a, Beck)

　b. What is the result so far as we are concerned? (vs 18b, Beck)

　c. Who is it who made this possible? (vs 18b)

　d. What did Christ do to make this possible? (vs 21a, compare Is. 53:6 and Lev. 16:21-22)

　e. What did Jesus do then? (vs 15a)

　f. For whom did He do this? (vs 15a and 19a)

　g. What comforting thought do we have because of this? (vs 19b)

　h. What work has Jesus given us in this respect? (vs 18b, 19c)

33a. What warning does Paul give us in 6:1? (Beck)

   b. What else does he tell us in 6:2b? (Beck)

Chapters 6:3-7:1

34a. Read vss 3-13. In a practical way what was Paul's aim as one of God's workers? (vs 3)

   b. How did he sum up the lives of the apostles in vs 10?

      1.

      2.

      3.

35a. Read vss 14-7:1. What rule does Paul lay down regarding our associations with other people in the world? (vs 14a)

   b. Why? (vs 15b)

36a. What does he say we Christians are? (vs 16b)

   b. What, therefore, must be our aim in life? (7:1)

Chapter 7

37a. Read vss 2-16. What did Paul say about his feelings towards the Christians in Corinth? (vs 3b)

   b. What else did he tell them?

      1. (vs 4a)

      2. (vs 4b)

38a. What was it that had given Paul such a big lift when he was feeling so discouraged? (vs 6)

   b. What good news had Titus brought? (vs 7b)

39a. How did Paul say he had felt about writing such a hot letter to them? (vs 8b)

   b. How did he feel now? (vs 9a)

   c. Why?

   d. What did he say about the people in Corinth now? (vs 11, last sentence)

Chapters 8-9

40a. Read 8:1-15. What was Paul talking about here? (See I Cor. 16:1-4)

  b. Whom did he use as a good example for the people in Corinth to follow? (vs 1)

  c. What did he say about them? (vs 3)

  d. What does Paul suggest as the first principle for Christian giving? (vs 5b)

41a. What compliment did Paul pay the Christians in Corinth? (vs 7a)

  b. What appeal did he then make? (vs 7c, Beck, RSV)

  c. What was another reason for asking them to do this? (vs 10b)

42a. What is the only true motivation for Christian giving? (vs 9a)

  b. Why is Jesus such a perfect example for us? (vs 9b)

43a. How does God feel about our gifts? (vs 12a)

  b. What story is the best illustration of this? (Luke 21:1-4)

  c. At the time Paul wrote this letter, what was the situation of the people in Corinth? (vs 14a, RSV)

44. Read 8:16-24. Why did Paul want to take men from all the congregations to bring their gifts to Jerusalem? (vs 20)

45a. Read 9:1-15. What compliment did Paul pay the Corinthians in vs 2?

  b. What did Paul say he was concerned about? (vss 3b-4a, 5b)

46a. What practical principles must we follow in our Christian giving?

    1. (vs 7a)

    2. (vs 7b)

  b. What two things must we remember about God as we give to Him?

    1. (vs 7c)

    2. (vss 8 and 11)

LESSON 21 - ACTS 20:2-3; ROMANS 1-7

Paul Goes to Corinth and Writes a Letter to the Christians in Rome
Winter, 57 A.D.

Acts 20

1a. Read vs 2-3. Where did Paul go now? (vs 2b)

b. How long did he stay there? (vs 3a)

Romans (Written during this time)

Chapter 1

2a. Who wrote this letter? (vs 1a)

b. To whom did he write it? (vs 7a)

c. What did he call these people? (vs 7b, see Lesson 6, question 12a)

3a. What had God called Paul to be? (vs 1b, Beck)

b. What is the Gospel all about? (vs 3a and 4b, last four words)

4a. Read vss 8-17. What nice thing did Paul say about the Christians in Rome? (vs 8b)

b. What else did he tell them?

   1. (vs 9b, KJ, RSV, 9b-10a, NIV)

   2. (vs 10)

   3. (vs 13a)

5. What did Paul wish to do there in Rome? (vs 15)

6a. What did Paul say the Gospel is? (vs 16b)

b. What is there in the Gospel that brings a person salvation? (vs 17a)

c. What is "righteousness"? (See Matt. 5:48)

d. What has made it possible for us sinners to become perfect in God's sight? (see Isaiah 53:6 and II Cor. 5:21a).

e. How do we receive this "imputed" righteousness? (vs 17b)

7a. Read vss 18-31. How does Paul describe the world of men and women in this section? (vs 18a and 29a, very briefly)

b. What has this done so far as God is concerned? (vs 18a)

Chapter 2

8a. Read vss 1-6. What sin is Paul writing about here? (vs 1a, RSV, NIV)

b. What does he say about the people who do this? (vs 1b)

c. Why? (vs 1c)

d. What will happen to such people? (vs 5)

9. Read vss 7-16. Of what truth does Paul remind us in vs 11? (NIV, RSV)

10a. Who were the people in Paul's day who didn't have the Law? (vss 9 and 10, last word)

b. What will happen to them on Judgment Day? (vs 12a)

c. On what basis will God judge them? (vs 14b)

d. Who were the people who had the Law? (vs 12b, see 9b and 10b)

e. On what basis will they be judged? (vs 13b, compare Luke 10:25-28, especially the last phrase)

11a. Read vss 17-29. What question did Paul ask the Jews? (vs 23b)

b. Under what circumstances would circumcision be of value? (vs 25a)

12a. What was Paul's definition of a real Jew? (vs 29a, compare Ezek. 36:26)

b. Who is it who works this change in a person? (vs 29b, compare John 3:5)

Chapter 3

13. Read vss 1-8. What advantage did the Jews have? (vs 2b)

14a. Read vss 9-20. Did the Jews have any other advantages over other people? (vs 9a)

   b. What had Paul proven in chapters 1-2? (vs 9b; RSV, vs 10)

   c. What is the value of the Law so far as being justified, or regarded as perfect in God's sight is concerned? (vs 20a)

   d. What, then, is the primary purpose of the Law? (vs 20b)

15a. Read vss 21-31. Where has God's righteousness or way of becoming perfect been revealed? (vs 21a, compare 1:17)

   b. What does this have to do with the Law? (vs 21b)

   c. Who may have this righteousness? (vs 22b-24)

16a. Who is it who has removed our sins and made this possible? (vss 24-25a)

   b. How, then, does a person become righteous in God's sight? (vs 28)

Chapter 4

17a. Read vss 1-12. Whom does Paul use as an example of what he has just said? (vs 1)

   b. What do the Scriptures say about him? (vs 3)

   c. What was Abraham's condition when this happened? (vs 10)

   d. What was the purpose or meaning of circumcision? (vs 11a, RSV, NIV)

18a. What, then, is Abraham's relationship to the gentiles? (vs 11b)

   b. What is his relationship to the Jews? (vs 12a)

   c. But how is this relationship narrowed down? (vs 12b)

19a. Read vss 13-25. How did God make His covenant with Abraham in Gen. 12:1-3?

   1. (vs 13a) Not...

   2. (vs 13b) But...

b. How, then, does our inheritance come to us? (vs 16a)

c. What comfort does this bring to us gentiles? (vs 16b)

    It is guaranteed...

d. What did God say to Abraham which told him the same thing? (vs 17a)

20. How does Paul sum up Jesus' work on our behalf? (vs 25)

    1.

    2.

Chapter 5

21. Read vss 1-11. So far as we are concerned, what are the results of the fact that God has accepted us as perfect?

    1. (vs 1)

    2. (vs 2a)

    3. (vs 2b)

22a. What else do we boast about? (vs 3a)

  b. Why? (NIV)

    1. (vs 3b)

    2. (vs 4a)

    3. (vs 4b)

23a. What is so remarkable about the fact that Christ died for us?

    1. (vs 6a)

    2. (vs 6b)

    3. (vs 8)

    4. (vs 10)

  b. What assurance does this give us? (vs 9b)

24a. Read vss 12-21. How did sin come into the world? (vs 12a)

  b. To what event does this refer? (See Gen. 3:1-6)

  c. What did sin bring with it? (vs 12b)

d. What was the result of all this? (vs 12c)

e. Why? (vs 12d)

25a. Of whom is Adam a type, or picture? (vs 14b)

b. What is the difference between the effects of the work these two men have done?

    1. (vs 16b)

    2. (vs 16c)

c. How else does Paul describe this difference? (vs 17)

    1.

    2.

d. How does Paul compare their work in vs 18?

    1.

    2.

e. How does Paul compare the work of Adam and Jesus in vs 19?

    1.

    2.

26a. Why did God give the Law at a later date? (vs 20a)

b. What other lesson, however, do we learn from this? (vs 20b)

Chapter 6

27a. Read vss 1-14. If God's love and willingness to forgive is so abundant, what would the average person say? (vs 1)

b. Why is it impossible for us Christians to go on living in sin? (vs 2b)

c. When did we die to sin? (vs 3)

d. What is the ultimate purpose of our baptism? (vs 4b)

28a. What assurance do we have from our baptism? (vs 5b)

b. Of what else does our baptism assure us? (vs 6b, KJ, RSV)

    1.

    2.

29. How must we think of ourselves as Christians? (vs 11b)

30a. Read vss 15-23. What is another reason why we can't go on sinning? (vss 17-18, briefly)

b. What is our present condition? (vs 22a)

31a. What is the result of serving Satan and sin? (vs 23a)

b. What is the result of serving God? (vs 23b)

Chapter 7

32a. Read vss 1-6. What legal principle does Paul quote here? (vs 1b)

b. What example of this does he give? (vs 2)

    1.

    2.

33a. What happened, then, at our baptism? (vs 4a)

b. What does this mean, therefore? (vs 4b)

c. Who rules our life now? (vs 6b)

34. Read vss 7-25. What purpose does the Law serve? (vs 7)

35a. What, however, is our real condition at the present time? (vs 14b, RSV)

b. What does Paul say about our old sinful nature? (vs 18a)

36. What does this mean so far as our everyday lives are concerned? (vs 15b)

    1.

    2.

37. What is it which leads us to do all these bad things? (vs 17 and 20)

38. Who will rescue us from this dying body of ours? (vs 25a)

LESSON 22 - ROMANS 8-16
Winter, 57 A.D.

Chapter 8

1a. Read vss 1-5. What comforting thought begins this chapter? (vs 1)

 b. Why? (vs 2, compare 7:25b)

 c. How is this possible?

    1. (vs 3a, RSV)

    2. (vs 3b, RSV)

 d. What was the result of all this for us believers? (vs 4)

2a. Read vss 6-17. What does Paul say about the mind of the typical unbeliever? (vs 7a, Beck)

 b. What does this mean in a practical way? (vs 8)

3a. Why can the believer be sure that his life is not controlled by his sinful human nature, but by the Spirit? (vs 9a)

 b. What does the Spirit do for all believers? (vs 11b)

4a. What does this indwelling of the Spirit in us make of us? (vs 14)

 b. What else does this make us? (vs 17)

5. Read vss 18-39. What does Paul say about our present sufferings and troubles? (vs 18)

6a. What is the created world waiting for? (vs 19, NIV)

 b. What is their hope? (vs 21)

 c. And what about us believers? (vs 23)

7a. How does the Spirit help us in our troubles? (vs 26b)

 b. What confidence does this give us? (vs 28, KJ)

8. What other assurances do we have as Christians?

   1. (vs 29a)

   2. (vs 29b)

   3. (vs 30a)

   4. (vs 30b)

   5. (vs 30c)

9. What, then, should be our general attitude as Christians? (vs 31)

10. What special confidence do we have regarding Judgment Day?

    1. (vs 33)

    2. (vs 34)

11. What, then, can separate us from God's love which has come to us through Christ? (vss 35-39)

Chapter 9

12. Read vss 1-5. How did Paul feel about his fellow Jews? (vs 2)

13a. What had God done for the Jews? (vs 4b, see Ex. 19:5-6)

  b. What had God given them? (vs 4c)

     1.   3.   5.

     2.   4.

  c. In what other two ways were the Jews distinguished from all other nations?

     1. (vs 5a)

     2. (vs 5b)

14. Read vss 6-13. What two strange sounding truths does Paul reveal in vss 6b-7a? (NIV)

    1.

    2.

15a. What promise did God give Abraham? (vs 7b)

b. What similar promise did God give Rebecca? (vs 12b)

   c. Why did God choose Isaac and Jacob? (See 4:12b and Gal. 3:7)

   d. Who, then, is "Israel" in God's sight?

      1. (vss 8a and 7a) It isn't Abraham's...

      2. (4:12b and Gal. 3:7) but those who...

16a. Read vss 14-33. Is God unfair when He makes such choices? (vs 14b)

   b. How does Paul answer this question in 21a?

   c. What example did Paul give? (vss 17-18, 22-23, briefly)

17a. What was the result of all these actions by God?

      1. (vs 30)

      2. (vs 31)

   b. Read 10:1-4. How does Paul sum all this up in 10:4?

Chapter 10

18. Read vss 5-13. What is wrong with the Law's way of making us perfect in God's sight? (vs 5, compare 3:23 and 3:20a, and put in your own words)

19a. How does Paul sum up God's way of becoming perfect in vs 9?

   b. What wonderful promise, or offer, does God make in His way of salvation? (vs 12b)

20. Read vss 14-21. What plan was God following to tell people about His way of salvation? (vs 15a)

21. What was Israel's problem? (vs 21b, see Is. 65:2)

Chapter 11

22a. Read vss 1-10. Has God rejected His chosen people? (vs 1a, 2a)

   b. What example does Paul give in vss 2b-4?

   c. How many faithful Israelites were there left at that time? (vs 4)

23. What did Paul say the situation was in his day?

    1. (vs 5)

    2. (vs 7)

24a. Read vss 11-24. What was the result of Israel's rejection? (vs 11b)

  b. What does Paul suggest is going to happen later? (vss 12b, 15b, 23)

25a. Read vss 25-36. What was the secret Paul told the people in Rome? (vs 25a, RSV, Beck)

  b. How long would this hardening last? (vs 25b)

  c. What, then, would be the final result? (vs 26a)

  d. Who would be included in "all Israel"? (See 9:6b, 24, 30; and 11:5b and 23; and question 15d)

Chapter 12

26a. Read vss 1-20. What does Paul ask us to do because of God's mercies to us? (vs 1a)

  b. What do we call such service to God? (vs 1b, last 3 words, NIV)

27a. What must be our relationship to the world? (vs 2a)

  b. What must happen to us? (vs 2b)

28. What advice does Paul give us in vs 3?

    1. (vs 3a)

    2. (vs 3b, Beck)

29a. What example does Paul use in his discussion in vss 4-8? (vs 4a)

  b. How does he describe the Christian church here?

    1. (vs 5a)

    2. (vs 5b)

    3. (vs 6a)

c. What is he telling us in vss 6b-8? (Sum up briefly)

30. How does Paul sum up all these instructions in vss 9-21? (vs 9a)

Chapter 13

31. Read vss 1-14. Sum up briefly what Paul says here about our relationship to the state. (vs 1a)

32a. What should be our only debt as Christians? (vs 8a)

b. What does he say about our Christian love? (vss 8b and 10b)

33a. What kind of sins is Paul warning us against in vss 11-13? (See Gal. 5:19 and Eph. 2:3, RSV, Beck)

b. What must be our aim in our Christian lives? (vs 14a)

Chapters 14-15:13

34a. Read 14:1-14. What must we do for those whose faith is weak? (vs 1a)

b. How does Paul describe such people?

    1. (vs 2b)

    2. (vs 5a)

c. What other instructions does Paul give us? (vs 3a)

35. What about the one whose faith is weak? (vs 3b)

36a. What principle, or general rule, does Paul lay down in vs 7a?

b. How does this apply to us as Christians?

    1. (vs 8a)

    2. (vs 8b)

37a. Of what other important truth does Paul remind us in vs 10b?

b. In view of this, how must we act? (vs 13)

    1.

    2.

c. What truths must we keep in mind in this respect? (vs 14)

    1.

2.

   d. Read 14:15-15:6. What does all this mean for us?

      1. (vs 15a, RSV, Beck)

      2. (vs 19)

      3. (vs 21)

      4. (15:1)

38a. How is all this summed up in 15:2?

  b. Who is the great example of this? (vs 3)

39a. What is one of the reasons God has caused the Scriptures to be written? (vs 4a)

  b. What is one of the results He wants to see in us? (vs 4b)

40. Read vss 7-13. What rule does God lay down for both Jews and gentiles? (vs 7)

<u>apters 15:14-16:27</u>

  a. Read 15:14-33. What was Paul's aim in his work as an apostle? (vs 20)

  b. Why?

  c. How had this affected the people in Rome? (vs 22)

42a. What were Paul's plans now? (vs 24a and 28)

  b. Where was he going first? (vs 25)

  c. Why? (See II Cor. 9:1-5, 12-15)

43. What did he ask the people in Rome to do now? (vs 30)

44. Read 16:1-27. Who was the person who carried this letter to Rome? (vs 1a)

45. What final instructions did Paul give them? (vs 17)

46. What were Paul's wishes for his brethren in Rome? (vs 19b)

47. What was the name of the secretary who wrote this letter for Paul? (vs 22)

LESSON 23 - ACTS 20:3-23:11

Paul Returns to Jerusalem and is Arrested

May, 57 A.D.

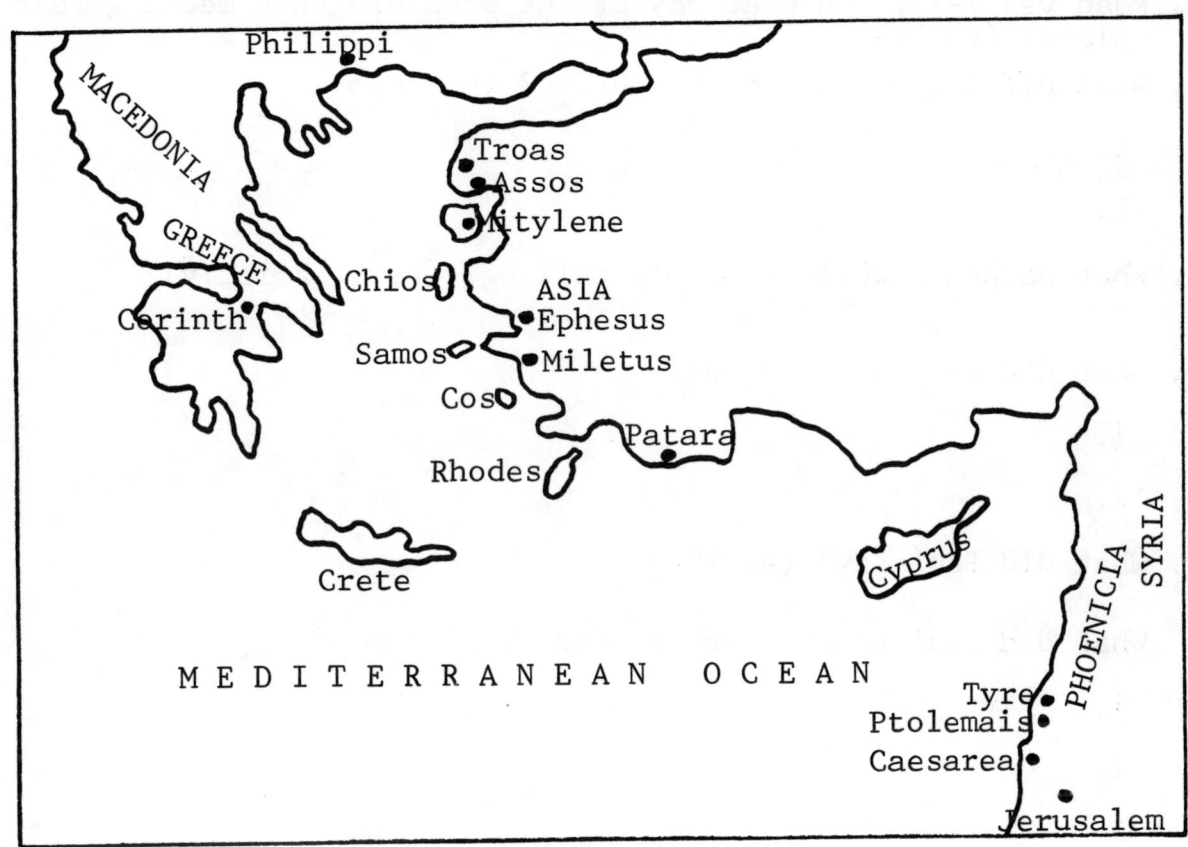

Chapter 20

1a. Read vss 1-6. Where was Paul at this time? (vs 2b, see 18:1)

b. What happened during his stay there? (vs 3b)

c. Where was Paul going to go next? (Rom. 15:25)

d. What did he do when he found out about the plot? (vs 3c)

e. Who went along with him? (vs 4)

    1.   4.   6.

    2.   5.   7.

    3.

f. Who else joined the group in Philippi? (See 1st word in vs 6; and Lesson 14, question 14c)

g. When did they leave Philippi? (vs 6a, see note in Good News)

2a. What was their first stop? (vs 6b, locate on map)

 b. How long did they stay there? (vs 6c)

3a. Read vss 7-12. On what day of the week did this meeting take place? (vs 7a)

 b. What did they do at their meeting? (vs 7a)

   1.

   2.

4a. What happened while Paul was talking? (vs 9, briefly)

 b. What did Paul do? (vs 10a)

   1.

   2.

 c. What did Paul say? (vs 10b)

5. What did Paul do after this? (vs 11)

   1.

   2.

   3.

6. Read vss 13-16. Outline their journey from Troas. (vss 13-15, trace on map)

   1.   3.   5.

   2.   4.

7. Why did Paul bypass Ephesus? (vs 16)

8. Read vss 17-38. What did Paul do when he arrived in Miletus? (vs 17)

9a. What did he tell them about his work there in Asia? (vs 20a)

 b. What did he say about his present plans? (vs 22a)

 c. What had the Holy Spirit told him was going to happen there? (vs 23)

 d. What did he tell the group then? (vs 25)

10a. What did he call the elders to whom he was talking? (vs 28b)

   b. What instructions did he give them? (vs 28a)

11. What else did he tell them?

    1. (vs 29)

    2. (vs 30)

12. What happened when he finished his speech?

    1. (vs 36)

    2. (vs 38b)

Chapter 21

13. Read vss 1-16. Outline their journey from Miletus. (vs 1-3, trace on map)

    1.   3.   5.

    2.   4.

14a. What did they do in Tyre? (vs 4a)

   b. How long did they stay there? (vs 4a)

   c. What did they tell Paul? (vs 4c)

15a. Where did they go next? (vs 7a, locate on map)

   b. Where did they go the next day? (vs 8a, locate on map)

   c. Where did they stay there? (vs 8b)

   d. How long did they stay there? (vs 10a)

16a. Who else came to town while Paul was there? (vs 10b)

   b. What message did he give Paul? (vs 11b, your own words)

17. What did Paul say when they begged him not to go to Jerusalem? (vs 13b)

18a. Who else went with Paul when they left town? (vs 16a)

b. Where did Paul stay in Jerusalem? (vs 16b)

19a. Read vss 17-26. What kind of a reception did Paul receive there? (vs 17)

b. What did Paul do the next day? (vs 18a)

c. Who was James? (See note at 12:17 in the Good News)

d. Who else was present? (vs 18b)

20. What did Paul talk to them about? (vs 19)

21. What information did they give to Paul?

    1. (vs 20b)

    2. (vs 21)

    3. (vs 22b)

22. What did they suggest should be done about this?

    1. (vs 23b)

    2. (vs 24a)

    3. (vs 24b, to "shave their heads")

    4. (vs 24c)

23. What did they say about the believers who weren't Jews? (vs 25)

24. What did Paul do, therefore?

    1. (vs 26a)

    2. (vs 26b)

25a. Read vss 27-36. What happened next? (vs 27, briefly)

b. What did they accuse Paul of doing?

    1. (vs 28a)

2. (vs 28b)

c. What was the crowd trying to do? (vs 31a)

26a. Who stopped them from doing so? (vss 31-32)

b. What did he do?

1. (vs 33a, to "chains")

c. (vs 34b, last phrase)

c. What did the crowd do? (vs 36)

27. Read vss 37-40. What request did Paul make of the colonel? (vs 39b)

Chapter 22

28a. Read vss 1-21. Of what facts did Paul remind the people?

1. (vs 3b)

2. (vs 3c)

3. (vs 3d, RSV, Beck)

4. (vs 4a)

b. What did he tell them about next?

1. (vss 6-10, briefly, your own words)

2. (vss 11-16, especially vs 16b)

c. What orders did God give Paul when he returned to Jerusalem? (vss 17-21, especially 18)

29. Read vss 22-29. What did the crowd do as soon as he mentioned the gentiles? (vs 22a, Beck)

30. What orders did the colonel give then?

1. (vs 24a)

2. (vs 24b)

31a. What question did Paul ask the centurion as they were about to begin? (vs 25b)

b. What happened when they found out Paul was a Roman citizen?

    1. (vs 29a)

    2. (vs 29b)

Chapters 22:30-23:11

32a. Read 22:30. What did the colonel want to know? (vs 30a)

  b. What did he do?

    1. (vs 30b)

    2. (vs 30c)

33a. Read 23:1-11. What information does Luke give us about the Sanhedrin? (vs 6a)

  b. How did Paul begin his defense?

    1. (vs 6b)

    2. (vs 6b)

    3. (vs 6c)

34a. What happened then? (vs 7)

  b. What were some of the differences between the two groups?

    1. (vs 8a)

    2. (vs 8b)

    3. (vs 8c)

35a. Who were the first ones to speak? (vs 9a)

  b. What did they say? (vs 9b)

36a. What was the colonel afraid of now? (vs 10a)

  b. What did he do? (vs 10b)

37. What did the Lord tell Paul that night? (vs 11)

    1.

    2.

LESSON 24 - ACTS 23:12-26:32

Paul Escapes from the Jews and is Imprisoned in Caesarea

May, 57, A.D.

Chapter 23

1a. Read vss 12-15. What happened the next morning? (vss 12-13, briefly)

b. Who else did they bring into their plot? (vs 14a)

c. What plan of action did they propose?

    1. (vs 15a, Beck, NIV)

    2. (vs 15b)

2a. Read vss 16-22. Who overheard this conversation? (vs 16a)

b. What happened then?

    1. (vs 16b)

    2. (vs 17)

    3. (vs 18a)

    4. (vss 19-21, briefly)

3. Read vss 23-35. What did the colonel do?

    1. (vss 23-24, briefly)

    2. (vss 25-26)

4. What did the governor do when he read the letter?

    1. (vs 34)

    2. (vs 35a)

    3. (vs 35b)

Chapter 24

5a. Read vss 1-9. What happened next? (vs 1a)

 b. What did they do? (vs 1b)

6a. What happened after Paul was brought in? (vs 2a)

 b. What points did Tertullus mention at the beginning of his speech?

    1. (vs 2b)

    2. (vs 2c)

    3. (vs 3)

7. What accusations did he bring against Paul?

    1. (vs 5a)

    2. (vs 5b)

    3. (vs 5c)

    4. (vs 6a)

8a. Read vss 10-21. What was Paul's answer to these accusations?

    1. (vs 12a)

    2. (vs 12b)

    3. (vs 13)

 b. What did Paul say next?

    1. (vs 14a)

    2. (vs 14b)

    3. (vs 15)

9a. How did Paul explain his presence in the Temple-grounds? (vs 17)

 b. What did he say about his arrest? (vs 18b)

 c. Who did he say had started the trouble? (vs 19a)

d. What good point did he make then? (vs 19b)

e. What statement from his former trial did he then repeat? (vs 21b)

10a. Read vss 22-27. What announcement did Felix make then? (vs 22)

  b. What orders did he give?

    1. (vs 23a)

    2. (vs 23b)

11a. What happened a few days later? (vs 24a)

  b. What did Paul talk about this time?

    1. (vs 24b)

    2. (vs 25a)

12a. What effect did this have on Felix? (vs 25b)

  b. What did he tell Paul? (vs 25c)

  c. What was he hoping? (vs 26a)

  d. What did this lead him to do? (vs 26b)

13a. How long was Paul kept in prison there in Caesarea? (vs 27a)

  b. What happened at the end of this time?

    1. (vs 27a)

    2. (vs 27b)

Chapter 25

14a. Read vss 1-12. What did Festus do as soon as he arrived in his new district? (vs 1)

  b. What happened when he got there? (vs 2)

15a. What request did the Jewish leaders make? (vs 3a)

  b. What was their plan? (vs 3b)

16. What was Festus' answer?

    1. (vs 4a)

    2. (vs 4b)

    3. (vs 5)

17a. How long did Festus stay in Jerusalem? (vs 6a)

  b. What happened as soon as he got back to Caesarea? (vs 6b)

18. What did the Jews do when the trial opened? (vs 7)

19. What was Paul's answer? (vs 8)

    1.

    2.

    3.

20a. What was Festus planning to do? (vs 9a)

  b. What question did he ask Paul? (vs 9b)

21. What was Paul's answer?

    1. (vs 10a)

    2. (vs 10b)

    3. (vs 11a)

    4. (vs 11b)

    5. (vs 11c)

22. What was Festus' answer? (vs 12)

23. Read vss 13-22. What happened next? (vs 13)

24a. What did Festus do while they were there? (vs 14a, see also 14b-19)

b. What did Festus say his problem was? (vs 20a)

25a. What did Agrippa say? (vs 22a)

b. What was Festus' reply? (vs 22b)

26a. Read vss 23-27. Who attended the hearing the next day?

    1. (vs 23a)

    2. (vs 23b)

    3. (vs 23c)

b. What was Festus hoping to accomplish by this hearing? (vs 26b)

Chapter 26

27a. Read vss 1-8. Who was in charge of the hearing? (vs 1a)

b. Why was Paul happy to have the opportunity to plead his case before Agrippa? (vs 3a)

28a. What point did Paul emphasize in vss 4-5? (vs 5b)

b. What question did Paul then ask the people who were listening to him? (vs 8)

29. Read vss 9-18. What did Paul talk about next in vss 9-11? (Briefly, see last phrase in vs 11)

30. What did he talk about in the rest of this section (vss 12-18)? (briefly, see especially vs 14a)

31a. Read vss 19-23. What was his main point in this section? (vs 19)

b. To what groups of people had he gone as the Lord's apostle? (vs 20a)

    1.

    2.

    3.

c. How did Paul summarize his message? (vs 20b)

      1.

      2.

   d. What information did he add in vs 21?

   e. What special point did he make in vs 22b?

   f. And how did he sum up the message of Moses and the prophets in the Old Testament?

      1. (vs 23a)

      2. (vs 23b)

      3. (vs 23c)

32a. Read vss 24-32. What did Festus think of this speech? (vs 24)

  b. What was Paul's answer? (vs 26a)

33a. What did Agrippa reply when Paul asked him if he believed the prophets? (vs 28)

  b. What was Paul's answer? (vs 29)

34. How did all the people feel after they had heard Paul's speech? (vs 31b)

35. What was Agrippa's decision? (vs 32)

LESSON 25 - ACTS 27-28

Paul Goes to Rome and Stays Two Years as a Prisoner Awaiting Trial
59-62 A.D.

Chapter 27

1a. Read vss 1-8. What arrangements did the governor make to get Paul to Rome? (vs 1)

 b. Who else went with Paul?

   1. (See "we" in vs 1)

   2. (vs 2b)

 c. How did the trip start? (vs 2a)

2a. Where was their first stop? (vs 3a, locate on map)

 b. What kindness did Julius show to Paul? (vs 3b)

3a. Outline their journey from Sidon. (vss 4-5, trace on map)

   1. (vs 4)

   2. (vs 5a)

   3. (vs 5b)

 b. What happened at Myra? (vs 6)

4a. How far west did they get after leaving Myra? (vs 7a)

 b. Where did they go then? (vs 7b)

 c. Where did they finally land? (vs 8b)

5a. Read vss 9-15. What time of year was it now? (vs 9, see footnote in Good News and Beck)

 b. What did this mean so far as the voyage was concerned? (vs 9)

 c. What warning did Paul give the group? (vs 10, Good News, Beck)

 d. Who else expressed their opinions? (vs 11)

 e. What did the group decide to do? (vs 12a)

 f. Why? (vs 12a)

 g. Where did they hope to spend the winter? (vs 12b)

6a. What happened after some few days? (vs 13a)

 b. What did they do? (vs 13b)

7a. What happened very shortly? (vs 14)

 b. What was the situation then? (vs 15a)

 c. What did they do? (vs 15b)

8a. Read vss 16-26. What was the next bit of land they saw? (vs 16a)

 b. What did the ship's captain do then? (vs 16a)

 c. What did they accomplish by doing this? (vss 16b-17a, Good News, RSV)

 d. What else did they do as a safety measure? (vs 17b)

9a. What were they afraid of now? (vs 17c, Good News, Beck, NIV)

b. What did they do to prevent this? (vs 17c, Beck)

10a. What did they do the next day? (vs 18)

b. What did they do the day after that? (vs 19)

11a. What was the situation for the next several days?

    1. (vs 20a)

    2. (vs 20b)

b. How did the people on board feel? (vs 20b)

12a. How did the people act during this time? (vs 21a)

b. What advice did Paul give them? (vs 22a)

c. Why? (vs 22b)

d. How did Paul know this? (vss 23-24, briefly)

13. What other information did Paul give them? (vs 26)

14a. Read vss 27-44. How long had it been now since the storm started? (vs 27a)

b. What happened in the middle of the night? (vs 27b)

15a. What did they do?

    1. (vs 28a)

    2. (vs 28b)

    3. (vs 29b)

b. Why? (vs 29a)

16a. What happened next? (vs 30)

b. What warning did Paul give the others? (vs 31)

c. What did the soldiers do then? (vs 32)

17a. What did Paul do as the dawn was approaching? (vs 33-34a)

   b. What did they do after they had eaten? (vs 38)

   c. How many people were on the ship? (vs 37a)

18a. What happened when it got light? (vs 39)

   1.

   2.

   b. What did they do then?

   1. (vs 40a)

   2. (vs 40b)

   3. (vs 40c)

19. What happened next?

   1. (vs 41a)

   2. (vs 41b)

20a. What did the soldiers decide to do now? (vs 42)

   b. What did the captain do and why? (vs 43a)

   c. What orders did he give?

   1. (vs 43b)

   2. (vs 44a)

   d. How did it all turn out? (vs 44b)

Chapter 28

21a. Read vss 1-10. What was the name of the island on which they landed? (vs 1, locate on map)

   b. How did the natives receive them?

   1. (vs 2a)

   2. (vs 2b)

22a. What did Paul do? (vs 3a)

   b. What happened when he threw the sticks on the fire? (vs 3b)

23a. What did the natives think when they saw this? (vs 4b)

   b. What did they think was going to happen? (vs 6a)

24a. What did Paul do about it? (vs 5)

   b. What happened when he didn't die? (vs 6b)

25a. What happened next? (vs 7b)

   b. What did Paul do for him? (vs 8)

26a. What happened after this? (vs 9)

   b. What did the people of Malta do when Paul left? (vs 10)

27a. Read vss 11-16. How long did they stay on Malta? (vs 11a)

   b. Outline their journey from there? (vss 12-14, trace on map)

        1. (vs 12)

        2. (vs 13a)

        3. (vs 13b)

        4. (vs 14)

   c. What did the brothers in Rome do when they heard Paul was coming? (vs 15a, Good News)

28. What arrangements were made for Paul's imprisonment there in Rome? (vss 16 and 30a)

29. Read vss 17-31. What did Paul do shortly after he arrived? (vs 17a)

30. What did he say to them when they arrived?

        1. (vs 17b)

2. (vs 17c, Good News, Beck, RSV)

3. (vs 18)

4. (vs 19)

5. (vs 20b)

31a. What did the Jews answer?

    1. (vs 21)

    2. (vs 22a)

    3. (vs 22b)

  b. What did they do then? (vs 23a)

32a. How many men came to the meeting? (vs 23b)

  b. What did Paul do at this meeting? (vs 23b)

  c. What was he trying to do? (vs 23c)

  d. What were the results of his long lecture? (vs 24)

33a. What words of Isaiah did he quote just before they left? (vss 26-27, see footnote in Good News, Beck, NIV)

  b. What was he telling those Jews who didn't believe? (vs 27b, Good News, Beck, substitute "you" for "they")

  c. What were Paul's closing words to them? (vs 28)

34a. How long did Paul stay in Rome as a prisoner? (vs 30a)

  b. What was he doing during this time?

    1. (vs 30b)

    2. (vs 31)

LESSON 26 - PHILEMON, COLOSSIANS, EPHESIANS

Paul Writes to the Christians in Asia

61 A.D.

Philemon (This letter was written during the two years in prison to Philemon, one of Paul's friends in Colossae. Onesimus was one of his slaves who had run away to Rome and thus had come in contact with Paul, who brought him to faith and then sent him back to Philemon with this letter).

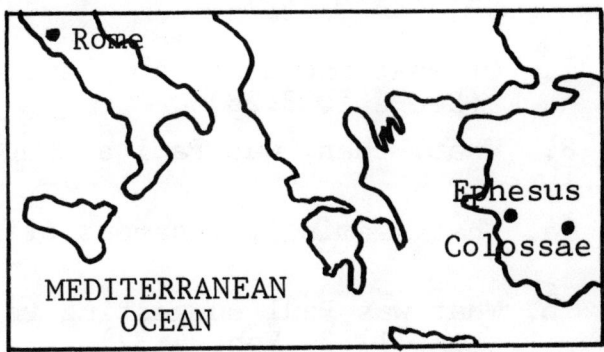

1. Read vss 1-3. To whom was the letter addressed? (vss 1-2)

    1.   2.   3.

    4.

2a. Read vss 4-7. What was Paul's opening thought? (vs 4)

 b. Why? (vs 5)

 c. What was Paul's prayer? (vs 6a, NIV)

3a. Read vss 8-21. What was Paul's reason in writing this letter? (vs 10a)

 b. In what sense had Paul become Onesimus' father? (vs 10b, see I Cor. 4:15)

 c. What did Paul say about Onesimus? (vs 11)

    1.

    2.

4a. What was Paul doing now? (vs 12a)

 b. What else did Paul say about this? (vs 13)

    1. (vs 13)

    2. (vs 14, NIV)

5. What did Paul say about the fact that Onesimus had run away? (vs 15)

6. But what was the situation now?

    1. (vs 16a)

    2. (vs 16b)

7. Of what fact was Paul reminding Philemon by saying this? (See Gal. 3:28)

8. What, then, was Paul asking Philemon to do? (vs 17)

9a. What seemingly generous offer did Paul make? (vs 18)

 b. What was Paul suggesting to Philemon by saying this? (See Luke 17:3, Eph. 4:32)

10. How did Paul close this request? (vs 21)

11a. What other request did Paul make? (vs 22a)

 b. Why? (vs 22b)

Colossians (This letter was written at the same time as Philemon, since Tychicus, who was sent to bring Onesimus back to Philemon, also carried the letter to the Christians in Colossae and Philemon's letter (Col. 4:7-9). Paul wrote this letter because the church in Colossae was having a problem. A religious group called Gnostics had come to town, and were turning the Christians away from Christ to a new kind of religion based on secret "knowledge" (gnosis). It was based on astrology, and they believed that all the heavenly bodies (sun, moon, stars), and angels and spirits were gods. It was like a modern secret society based on philosophy, astrology and horoscopes.)

12a. Read 1:1-2. Who wrote this letter? (vs 1)

 b. To whom did he address it? (vs 2)

13a. Read vss 3-14. For what was Paul thankful? (vs 4)

 b. What kind of knowledge did Paul want them to have? (vss 9b and 10, last 4 words, NIV, RSV)

 c. What benefits do we have as Christians?

    1. (vs 12b)

    2. (vs 14)

14a. Read vss 15-23. What two things did Paul emphasize about Christ?

    1. (vs 15)

    2. (vs 16, note that this includes all heavenly powers and spirits)

    3. (vs 18a)

    4. (vs 18c)

    5. (vs 19)

  b. What does Paul say Christ has done? (vs 20a)

  c. How did He do this? (vs 20b)

15. What must they do, therefore, to retain this salvation Christ has given them? (vs 23)

    1.

    2.

16a. Read 1:24-2:7. What did Paul say about the message of the Church in vs 26a.

  b. To whom had this mystery been revealed? (vs 26b)

  c. In what one word does Paul sum up this whole message? (vs 2:2b)

  d. Where are the treasures of wisdom and knowledge to be found? (vs 3)

  e. How does Paul sum up this section? (vs 6)

17a. Read 2:8-23. What warning did he sound in vs 8?

  b. What two important things did he then repeat?

    1. (vs 9)

    2. (vs 10)

18a. What did he caution them about in vs 16?

  b. What did he say about all these practices and ceremonies? (vs 17)

19a. Read 3:1-4:1. On what must we keep our eyes fixed? (3:1-2)

b. Of what great promise did he remind them in vs 4?

c. Read 3:5-14. Why must we avoid the sins of the flesh and live holy lives?
   1. (vs 9b)
   2. (vs 10)

d. What is the secret to such a Christian life? (vs 16a, first phrase)

e. What general rules did he lay down in 3:18-4:1?
   1. (vs 18)
   2. (vs 19)
   3. (vs 20)
   4. (vs 21a)
   5. (vs 22a)
   6. (vs 4:1a)

20a. Read 4:2-18. What request did Paul make in vs 3?

b. What instructions did he give in vs 16b? (Last phrase)

Ephesians (This letter was written at the same time as the other two, since the same man carried all three of them (see 6:21-22). It was not addressed to any one church, but to all the congregations in Asia, (see vs 1, RSV and Beck), and therefore it has no personal greetings at the end. It was written because these Gnostics had been busy in all these churches and it was a circular letter. Tychicus would read it first in Ephesus, and then it would be sent to all the other churches one by one. For a list of these churches, see Rev. 2-3. It is a warning against Gnosticism, and most of Colossians is repeated again here).

21a. Read 1:1-2. Who wrote this letter? (vs 1)

b. To whom did he address it? (vs 2, RSV, Beck, NIV footnote)

22a. Read vss 3-10. How does Paul sum up the whole section in vs 3?

b. How does he begin this summary of the Christian message? (vss 4-5)
   1. (vs 4)
   2. (vs 5)

c. What do we have because of Christ's work? (vs 7)

d. What did God do next? (vs 9a)

   e. What was God's ultimate aim in all this? (vs 10b)

23a. Read vss 11-14. Whom did God choose first? (vss 11-12, compare the "we" in vs 11 with Rom. 1:16a)

   b. Whom did He call after this? (vss 13-14, compare the "you" with 2:11a)

   c. What was the result God was looking for in both cases? (See the last phrases in vss 12 and 14)

24a. Read vss 15-23. What reason did Paul have for being thankful? (vs 15)

   b. What was Paul praying for? (vs 17, compare question 13b)

   c. What else was he praying for? (vs 18)

25a. What did God do for Christ after He raised Him from the dead? (vs 20b-21, compare with note in question 14a,2)

   b. What does this mean? (vs 22)

26a. Read 2:1-10. How does Paul describe our spiritual condition at the time of our birth? (vss 1 and 5a)

   b. What did the Holy Spirit do for us? (vs 5a)

   c. How does one receive this salvation?

      1. (vs 8c) through...

      2. (vs 9a) not by...

   d. What does Paul say about our faith? (vs 8b)

      1.

      2.

   e. For what purpose did God do all this for us? (vs 10)

27a. Read 2:11-22. What was the original condition of the gentiles? (vs 12)

      1.

      2.

3.

   b. What had Christ done for them? (vs 13)

   c. What was their situation now? (vs 19)

   d. On what were they built? (vs 20)

28. Read 3:1-21. What did Paul say the mystery was that had been kept secret for so long? (vs 6a)

29a. What is the only way we can approach God with freedom? (vs 12)

   b. What, then, was Paul's prayer for his readers?

      1. (vs 17a)

      2. (vs 18)

30a. Read 4:1-13. What must be our general aim as Christians? (vs 1)

   b. How does Paul emphasize the oneness of the Church in vss 4-6?

      There is 1.   4.   7.
                2.   5.
                3.   6.

31. What does Paul say about the individual Christians in the Church? (vs 7, Beck, see Rev. 12:6a)

32a. Read 4:20-5:14. What must we Christians strive to do?

      1. (4:22b)

      2. (4:24)

   b. What is to be our aim? (5:2a)

33a. How else does Paul describe our condition before we came to faith? (5:8a)

   b. What is our condition now as Christians? (5:8b)

34a. Read 6:10-18. Wherein does our strength lie as Christians? (vs 10)

   b. How can we protect ourselves against the devil and his forces? (vs 11a)

   c. What is our main weapon? (vs 17b)

LESSON 27 - PHILIPPIANS, I TIMOTHY, TITUS

Paul Writes to the Christians in Philippi, Timothy and Titus
61-62 A.D.

Philippians (This letter was written in 61 A.D., during Paul's 2-year imprisonment in Rome, to his most faithful and beloved congregation in Philippi (see map and Acts 16: 11-40). It does not deal with a lot of problems, like many of the other letters, but is just a happy personal letter to his friends, thanking them for their many gifts and letting them know how things are going.)

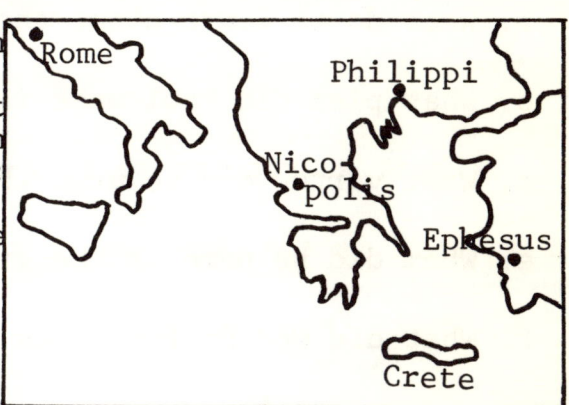

1a. Read 1:1-11. Who wrote this letter? (vs 1a)

  b. To whom did he address it? (vs 1b)

2a. What was Paul's reason for thanksgiving? (vs 5)

  b. What encouraging thought did he add in vs 6?

  c. How did Paul feel about the Christians in Philippi? (vss 7a, 8 and 4:1)

  d. What was his prayer for them? (vss 9-11)

   1. (vs 9)

   2. (vs 10)

   3. (vs 11)

3a. Read 1:12-26. What did Paul say about his imprisonment? (vs 12)

  b. Why? (vss 13-14)

   1.

   2.

  c. From what he says in vss 15-18, what was Paul's great aim in life? (vs 18b)

  d. What encouraging thought did he add in vs 19b? (Compare vs 25)

147

e. How did Paul feel as he looked forward to his trial? (vs 21)

4a. Read 1:27-2:18. What did Paul ask his friends to do in vs 27a?

b. What do we learn about the Christians in Philippi from vs 30a?

c. What plea did Paul make in 2:2?

d. What virtue did he urge them to cultivate in vs 3b?

e. Whom did he name as the great example of this virtue? (vs 5)

f. What did God do for Jesus because of His humility? (vs 9)

5. Where does the will or desire to do good works come from? (vs 13)

6. Read 2:19-3:1. Who was Epaphroditus? (2:25b)

7a. Read 3:2-21. Whom did Paul warn the Philippians about in 3:2-3a? (Compare Acts 15:5 and Gal. 5:2-6)

b. Whom did Paul say were truly circumcised? (vs 3)

c. Whom did Paul use as his example of one who used to put great confidence in his circumcision and efforts to keep the Law? (vss 4b-6)

d. What did Paul say about himself now? (vs 7)

e. What did he say is the greatest thing of all? (vs 8a)

f. What kind of righteousness did Paul want? (vs 9)

   1. not...

   2. but...

g. What three things did Paul want to know? (vs 10)

   1.   2.

   3.

h. What was Paul's ultimate purpose in life? (vs 14)

i. What is Christ going to do for us when He returns in glory? (vs 21a)

8. Read chapter 4. What kind of things should we fill our minds with? (vs 8)

9a. What did Paul say about the Christians in Philippi in vs 15b?

b. What was one reason Paul wrote this letter? (vs 18b)

<u>I Timothy</u> (This letter was written in 62 A.D., shortly after Paul was released from prison, following his trial at which he was found not guilty. Paul left Rome and went to Crete (see map), and after a short stay he left Titus to get the work organized and went on to Ephesus, and probably Colossae to see Philemon and Onesimus. Then he left Timothy at Ephesus to oversee the work there and hurried on to Philippi (see Phil. 2:24). Very soon after his arrival, he wrote this letter to Timothy to give him encouragement and instruction for his battle against the Gnostics (see Colossians and Ephesians).

10a. Read 1:1-2. Who wrote this letter? (vs 1)

b. To whom did he address it? (vs 2)

11a. Read 1:3-11. Why had Paul left Timothy in Ephesus? (vs 3b)

b. What kind of things were these men teaching? (vs 4a)

c. What had been the results of this? (vs 6)

d. On what particular doctrine or Bible teaching had some of the Christians been led astray? (vss 7-10, compare Col. 2:16)

12a. Read 1:12-20. Why did Jesus come into the world? (vs 15)

b. What must Timothy do in particular in his fight against the Gnostics? (vs 19a)

13a. Read 2:1-15. What was one thing Paul wanted the Christians to be doing? (vss 1 and 8)

b. What two things in particular does God want? (vs 4)

   1.

   2.

c. Who had made all this possible? (vs 5-6)

d. What does Paul call Jesus here? (vs 5)

14a. Read 3:1-16. How did Paul summarize all these qualifications for church officers? (vs 2a, first phrase)

   b. What does Paul call the Church in vs 15?

      1.

      2.

      3.

15a. Read 4:1-16. Of what did Paul remind Timothy in vs 1?

   b. What did he call the Gnostic teachers?

      1. (vs 1b)

      2. (vs 2a)

   c. What particular errors were they teaching the people? (vs 3a, compare Col. 2:21)

      1.

      2.

   d. What comforting thing does Paul say about Christians? (vs 10b)

16. What personal instructions did Paul give Timothy in vss 11-16?

      1. (vs 12b)

      2. (vs 13)

      3. (vs 16a)

17. Read 5:1-6:2. What was to be Timothy's rule in dealing with all the different kinds of people in Ephesus? (vs 21b)

18. Read 6:3-21. What did Paul say here about the Gnostic teachers?

      1. (vs 4a, NIV, Beck)

      2. (vs 5b, Beck)

19a. Of what truth did Paul remind his readers in vs 6?

   b. What must we remember when we think about material possessions? (vs 7)

c. What must our attitude be towards material things? (vs 8)

d. What does Paul say about those who want to be rich? (vs 9)

e. What does he say about the love of money? (vs 10a, NIV, Beck)

f. What instructions was Timothy to give to those who were rich? (vs 17)

    1. Not to

    2. but to

g. How were they to use their wealth? (vs 18)

h. What could they accomplish by doing this? (vs 19)

20. What did Paul say about the teachings of the Gnostics? (vs 20b)

Titus (This letter was also written from Philippi, a bit later than the letter to Timothy. Like the letter to Timothy, however, Paul's aim was to encourage Titus in his work of organizing the new congregations in Crete and establishing them in the true faith. It is clear that some Jewish Gnostics had begun their work there, as they had done earlier in Colossae (see Col. 2:16 and 20), and Paul instructs Titus how to deal with them. You will see that this letter is very similar to I Timothy)

21a. Read 1:1-4. Who wrote this letter? (vs 1a)

  b. What kind of knowledge did he say God had called him to make known? (vs 1b, RSV, Beck)

  c. Where is the true knowledge and truth revealed? (vs 3, RSV, Beck)

  d. To whom was the letter addressed? (vs 4)

22a. Read 1:5-16. Why had Paul left Titus in Crete? (vs 5, NIV, Beck)

    1.

    2.

  b. What was the main qualification for men chosen to be elders? (vs 6a, see question 14a)

23a. What was the nationality of the false teachers in Crete? (vss 10b, last phrase, and 14)

  b. What did Paul say about them in vs 16a?

24a. Read 2:1-15. What were Paul's general instructions to Titus?

    1. (vs 1)

    2. (vs 7a)

  b. What is our great blessed hope? (vs 13b)

  c. For what two purposes did Christ die? (vs 14)

    1.

    2.

25a. Read 3:1-15. What instructions was Titus to give the people about their everyday lives?

    1. (vs 1a)

    2. (vs 1b)

    3. (vs 2a)

    4. (vs 2b, NIV)

    5. (vs 2c, last phrase)

  b. Why did Christ save us? (vs 5a)

    1. not because of...

    2. but...

  c. What special means besides the Word did God use to save us? (vs 5b, Beck)

26. What were Paul's instructions about the false teachers? (vs 10)

    1.

    2.

    3.

27a. What special instructions did he send to Titus in vs 12a? (locate on map)

  b. From the location of Nicopolis, where was Paul apparently planning to go next? (See Rom. 15:24 and 28)

  c. Who carried this letter to Crete? (vs 13)

LESSON 28 - I PETER, II PETER, JUDE
63-70 A.D.

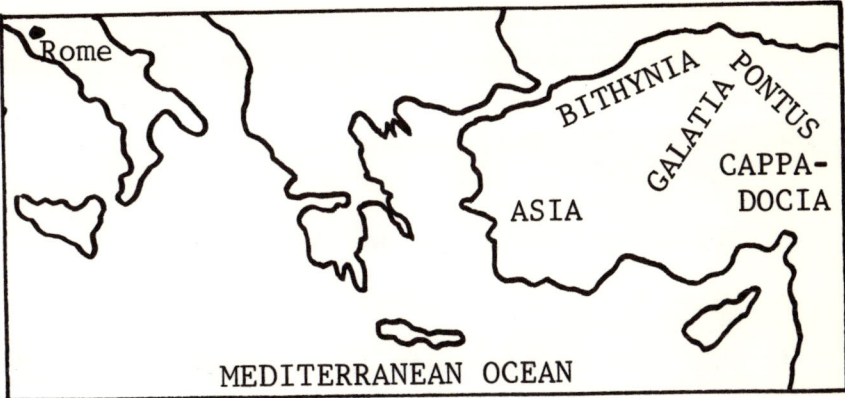

I Peter (This letter was written not long after Paul left Rome probably about 63 A.D., by Peter, who had recently come to Rome. His purpose was to encourage the Christians in some of the provinces of Asia Minor to hold on to their faith, since by this time they were suffering some form of persecution and abuse because of their faith).

1a. Read 1:1-2. Who wrote this letter? (vs 1a)

b. To whom did he address it? (vs 1b, locate on the map)

c. Of what did Peter remind his readers? (vs 2a)

d. Who was it who had brought them to faith? (vs 2b)

e. What did the Spirit wish to do for them now? (vs 2c)

    1.

    2. (Compare Eph. 5:26-27)

2a. Read 1:3-12. For what must we Christians praise God? (vs 3a, through "hope")

b. What is the source of this hope? (vs 3b)

c. What is it that we are looking forward to receiving? (vs 4)

3. What was happening to the Christians at that time? (vs 6, see also 3:16-17, 4:4 and 12-16)

4. What was God doing for them in all this through their faith? (vs 5)

5. What is God's purpose in bringing such trials upon us? (vs 7)

6a. How do we Christians feel about Christ?

    1. (vs 8a)

    2. (vs 8b)

b. How do we feel about our life, even though it is filled with troubles and sufferings? (vs 8c)

c. Why? (vs 9)

7. Where do we learn about this hope of ours? (vss 10-12, briefly)

8a. Read 1:13-2:3. How does Peter sum up the last paragraph in vs 13b?

b. Whose children are we now? (vs 14a, see 1:3)

c. What kind of children must we try to be? (vs 14a)

d. What does this mean in a practical way?

    1. (vs 14b)

    2. (vs 15)

9a. What is our relationship to the world in which we are now living? (vs 17, see also 2:11a)

b. What is it that Christ used to buy us back and set us free from the life of this world? (vss 18-19)

10a. How then do we purify ourselves? (vs 22a)

b. What must our relationship be with our fellow believers? (vs 22b)

11. What was it which brought about our new birth? (vs 23)

12a. What then is our present state or condition? (vs 2:2a)

b. What must we do as such?

    1. (vs 2:1)

    2. (vs 2:2, Beck, RSV)

13a. Read 2:4-10. What does Peter call Jesus in vs 4a?

b. What does he call us in vs 5a?

c. What is happening to us? (vs 5b)

14a. What position has God given us Christians? (vs 9a)

b. What therefore must we be doing? (vs 9b)

15a. Read 2:11-25. What must our general rules be for living in this world?

    1. (vs 12)

2. (vs 16a)

3. (vs 16b)

b. What did Peter say about the physical sufferings that may come to us? (vs 20)

1.

2. (See also 3:14 and 17, 4:15-16)

c. Who is the best example of this? (vs 21-25, compare 3:18)

d. What was the cause of His suffering? (vs 24a)

e. What was His purpose in doing this? (vs 24b)

16a. Read 3:1-7. What instructions did Peter give the wives? (vs 1a, compare Eph. 5:22-24)

b. What is one reason they should do this? (vss 1b-2)

c. What kind of beauty should they be concerned with? (vss 3-4)

17. What were his instructions to the husbands? (vs 7)

18a. Read 3:8-22. How should we treat our fellow Christians? (vs 8)

b. What should we do when someone does something bad to us? (vs 9a, see Luke 6:28-29)

c. What if someone asks us about our Christian hope? (vs 15)

19. Read 4:1-11. What is one reason the unbelievers insult us? (vs 4a)

20. Of what did Peter remind his readers in vs 7a?

21. What is another general rule we must follow? (vs 10)

22a. Read 4:12-19. How should we feel when we suffer or are insulted because we are Christians? (vs 13a)

b. Why? (vs 13b)

c. What must we do under such circumstances? (vs 19)

23a. Read 5:1-14. What advice did Peter give the elders in the congregations? (vs 2, to "willing" NIV, "willingly" RSV, Beck)

b. What promise did he make them? (vs 4)

24a. What instructions did Peter give the young men which applies to all of us? (vs 7)

b. What warning did he give them which also applies to us? (vs 8b)

c. How can we stand against the devil? (vs 9a)

25. What will God do for us if we stand firm in our sufferings? (vs 10b)

26a. Who helped Peter write this letter? (vs 12a, compare Acts 15:22, 32 and 40)

b. Who else was with Peter at this time? (vs 13b)

<u>II Peter</u> (This letter must have been written after 63 and before Peter's death in 65-67. We can thus date it about 65 or 66. Its tone and contents are very much like his first letter).

27a. Read 1:1-2. Who wrote this letter? (vs 1a)

b. To whom was it addressed? (vs 1b)

28a. Read 1:3-11. What has God given us believers? (vs 3a)

b. How? (vs 3b)

c. What wonderful promise did God give us? (vs 4b, RSV, Beck)

1.

2.

29a. What must we do therefore? (vs 10a)

b. How do we do this?

1. (vs 5)

2. (vs 6)

3. (vs 7)

30a. Read 1:12-21. What does Peter say about what he had told them earlier? (vs 16)

1.

2.

b. What was he referring to in vss 17-18 as one great example of this? (See Matt. 17:1-8 briefly)

31a. What is even more dependable than Peter's eye witness testimony? (vs 19a, KJ, Beck)

   b. How did the Scriptures come to be written? (vs 21, Beck)

      1. (vs 21a)

      2. (vs 21b)

32a. Read 2:1-22. What did Peter say about the nation of Israel in 2:1a?

   b. What prophecy did he make in 1b? (See also 1c-3)

   c. What examples did Peter give of God's holy anger falling on His people who had forsaken Him in the past?

      1. (vs 4)

      2. (vs 5)

      3. (vs 6)

   d. What did he say about the false prophets who were in their midst now? (vs 15)

33a. Read 3:1-18. Of what two things did Peter want to remind his readers? (vs 2)

      1.

      2.

   b. What did he say the false prophets and the people of the world would say to us Christians?

      1. (vs 4a)

      2. (vs 4b)

   c. Of what should these people be reminded?

      1. (vs 5)

      2. (vs 6)

   d. How will the present world be destroyed on the last Day? (vs 7)

   e. What must we remember about the time of the end? (vs 8)

   f. Why does God wait so long? (vs 9b)

g. How will the end come? (vs 10a)

h. How does Peter describe the end? (vs 10b)
   1.
   2.
   3. (Beck)
   4. (NIV)

34a. What kind of people must we be therefore? (vs 11, NIV)

  b. What are we looking forward to? (vs 13)

  c. What was Peter's final warning to us? (vs 17b)

  d. What was his final advice? (vs 18a)

Jude (All we can say about this letter is that it was written after II Peter, since it echoes the thoughts of II Peter 2. A probable date of about 70 A.D. is most likely)

35a. Read vss 1-2. Who wrote this letter? (vs 1a)

  b. Which James does he call his brother? (See James 1, Acts 15:13 and Gal. 1:19)

  c. What then was his relationship to Jesus? (Mark 6:3a)

  d. To whom was the letter addressed? (vs 2)

36a. Read vss 3-19. What was his purpose in writing? (vs 3b)

  b. Why was this necessary? (vs 4a)

  c. What were they doing? (vs 4b)
     1.
     2.

  d. What was at stake here? (vs 3a)

37. Read vss 20-25. What must his readers to do protect themselves against these men? (vs 20)

38. What did he say God would do for us Christians? (vs 24)
     1.
     2.

LESSON 29 - II TIMOTHY, HEBREWS 1-4:13

Paul Writes His Last Letter, and Apollos Writes to the Jews in Rome

66-69 A.D.

II Timothy (We know that after his release from prison in 62, Paul travelled, probably to Spain, and returned to Asia Minor, where he was arrested again, probably at Troas. He was again imprisoned in Rome. After a short while he wrote this second letter to his dear friend Timothy. So far as we know, it was his last letter, and must have been written about 66 or 67).

1a. Read 1:1-2. Who wrote this letter? (vs 1a)

 b. To whom is the letter addressed? (vs 2a)

2a. Read 1:3-5. What was Paul thanking God for at this time?

    1. (vs 4a, first phrase)

    2. (vs 5a, first phrase)

 b. What was Paul's reason for writing this letter? (vs 4b)

3a. Read 1:6-14. What did Paul want Timothy to do? (vs 6)

 b. What gift was Paul probably talking about here? (vss 7b-8a, see I Cor. 14:4b and 5b)

 c. What else did he ask Timothy to do? (vs 8b)

4a. Of what did Paul remind Timothy in vs 9a?

    1.   2.

 b. Why?

    1. Not because...

    2. but because...

 c. When did God work out all these plans? (vs 9c)

 d. How and when did God reveal all this to us? (vs 10a)

5. How did Paul sum up Christ's life and work in vs 10b?

    1.

    2.

6. How did Paul feel about his present imprisonment?

    1. (vs 12b)

    2. (vs 12c)

7. What did he ask Timothy to do in vs 13? (RSV, Beck)

8a. Read 1:15-18. What had happened recently? (vs 15)

 b. Who was the one exception besides Timothy? (vs 16)

9. Read 2:1-7. What was it that should make Timothy strong? (vs 1)

10. What was Timothy's task there in Ephesus? (vs 2)

11a. What must Timothy expect as a good soldier of Christ? (vs 3, RSV)

 b. What must Timothy's aim in life be? (vs 4)

12. Read 2:8-13. How did Paul sum up his message in vs 8?

13a. What do we know about Paul's condition at this time from vs 9a?

 b. What does he say about God's Word? (vs 9b)

14. Of what four great facts did Paul remind Timothy in vss 11-13?

    1.

    2.

    3.

    4.

15a. Read 2:14-26. What did Paul say to encourage Timothy? (vs 19a)

 b. What general truth must Timothy keep in mind? (vs 19b)

16. What kind of a tool must Timothy strive to be? (vs 21b)

17. What was Timothy to do to those who opposed him? (vs 25, RSV, Beck)

18a. Read 3:1-9. What warning did Paul give Timothy and the Christians in Ephesus? (vs 1)

b. What description did he give? (vs 2, first two phrases; vs 3, first phrase; vs 4, last phrase)

    1.

    2.   3.

    4.

19a. Read 3:10-17. What does Paul say about all true followers of Christ? (vs 12)

  b. What general picture does he give of the world just before the end? (vs 13)

20a. What must we do to protect ourselves? (vs 14a)

  b. Why? (vs 15a)

    Because what we have learned comes from...

21a. What does Paul say about the Scriptures in vs 16?

    1. (vs 16a, to God, RSV, Beck)

    2. (vs 16b)

  b. Why did God give the Scriptures? (vs 17)

22. Read 4:1-8. How does Paul sum up this paragraph in vs 2a? (first phrase)

23. What prophecy did Paul make about the Church in the time just before the End? (vs 3)

    1.

    2.

24a. What does Paul say about himself in vss 6-7?

    1. (vs 6)

    2. (vs 7)

  b. What was there waiting for him? (vs 8)

25a. Read 4:9-22. What request did he make of Timothy?

    1. (vs 9)

    2. (vs 21a)

b. Who was with Paul at this time? (vs 11)

c. Whom else did Paul want Timothy to bring along? (vs 11)

d. What else did he want Timothy to bring? (vs 13)

    1.   2.

26. What news did he send about his first hearing or trial?

    1. (vs 16)

    2. (vs 17a)

    3. (vs 17b)

27. What was Paul's final comfort? (vs 18a)

Hebrews (Nobody knows exactly who wrote this interesting letter but the best evidence we have points to Apollos (see Acts 18:24-28, I Cor. 1:12, 3:4-9, 16:12, Titus 3:13). He was a Jew, educated in both the Hebrew Scriptures and Greek rhetoric, and had been in close contact with Paul. He had travelled extensively among Paul's congregations in Ephesus, Corinth, Rome and Crete. The letter must have been written about 68 or 69. There is no author's introduction and greetings, as in most other letters).

28a. Read 1:1-3. How had God revealed Himself in the past? (vs 1)

b. How has He revealed Himself in these last days? (vs 2a)

29a. What does the writer say about Jesus?

    1. (vs 2b)

    2. (vs 2c)

    3. (vs 3a)

    4. (vs 3a)

    5. (vs 3b)

b. How does he describe the work of Christ in vs 3c?

c. Where is the Son now? (vs 3d, compare the Apostles' Creed, "and sitteth...")

30a. Read 1:4-14. What is Jesus' relation to the angels? (vs 4a)

  b. How has God made this clear? (vs 4b)

  c. What is this name which makes Him so superior? (vs 5)

  d. What else is there about the Son which makes Him superior?

     1. (vs 8, briefly)

     2. (vs 10)

     3. (vs 11)

  e. What then is the relation of the angels to Him? (vs 6)

31. What position do the angels serve in God's Kingdom? (vs 14)

32a. Read 2:1-4. What does this superiority of the Son mean to us? (vss 2-3a)

  b. Why? (vs 3b)

  c. What did God do to emphasize the superior position of His Son? (vs 4)

33a. Read 2:5-18. How does the writer sum up the previous chapter in vs 5?

  b. To what truth, however, does the writer point in vss 6-7a and 9a? (Compare 7a and 9a with Phil. 2:7-8)

  c. To what event does this point? (vs 14a, compare Luke 2:4-7, briefly)

  d. What was God's purpose in doing this? (vs 14b, see Gen. 3:15b)

  e. What else did Jesus accomplish by all this?

     1. (vs 15)

     2. (vs 17b)

34. Why, then, did Jesus have to become a true man?

     1. (vs 17a)

2. (vs 18b)

35. Read 3:1-6. What must we do, then? (vs 1)

36a. In what way was Jesus similar to Moses? (vs 2)

  b. But in what way were they different?

    1. (vs 5) Moses...

    2. (vs 6) Jesus...

  c. What then is Jesus' relation to Moses? (vs 3)

37a. Read 3:7-19. What is one thing the writer is warning us against here? (vs 12)

  b. What example does he give of this sin? (vss 7-9, 16-19, especially 16b-17a)

  c. What did God say to those people? (vss 11 and 18-19)

38a. Read 4:1-13. How does all this apply to us? (vss 1a and 9)

  b. What land is the writer referring to here as the place where we shall find our rest? (See 12:22, Phil. 3:20 and I Pet. 1:4)

  c. In what way is our situation similar to that of the people of Israel? (vs 2a)

39a. What happened to the Israelites? (vs 2b)

  b. What then was the final result? (vs 6b)

40a. What must we do then?

    1. (vs 7b, last phrase)

    2. (vs 11)

  b. Who will finally enter into that Sabbath rest? (vs 3)

LESSON 30 - HEBREWS 4:14-13:25
68-69 A.D.

1a. Read 4:14-5:10. What does the writer say about Jesus in vs 14a?

b. What does he say about Him in vs 15? (Beck)

    1.

    2.

    3.

c. Because we have such a Head Priest, what may we do? (vs 16a)

d. What will happen when we do this? (vs 16b)

2a. What is the first qualification for a Head Priest? (5:1a)

b. What are his two special duties? (5:1b)

    1.

    2.

c. Of what importance is the fact that He is a man? (5:2)

d. What is another result of the fact that he is a man? (5:3)

3a. What three things about Jesus make Him different from all other head priests?

    1. (5:5b)

    2. (5:6)

    3. (4:15c)

b. What therefore is Jesus' relation to all other head priests?

4a. Who appointed the head priests in Israel? (5:4)

b. Who appointed Jesus as our Head Priest? (5:5-6)

c. Where is He carrying on His work for us now? (4:14a)

5a. Read 5:11-6:12. What must we do to keep from falling away from the faith? (6:1a)

b. What are some of the elementary teachings of the Christian faith?

    1. (6:1b)

    2. (6:1b)

    3. (6:2)

    4. (6:2)

    5. (6:2)

    6. (6:2)

c. If we're going to become mature Christians, what doctrine must we become thoroughly familiar with? (5:13)

6a. Read 6:13-7:27. What is "the inner room behind the curtain" (the Most Holy Place) where Jesus has gone as our Head Priest? (6:19, see also 4:14a)

b. To what other head priest is Jesus compared rather than Aaron? (6:20b)

c. Who was this man? (7:1a)

    1.   2.

d. In these respects how was Jesus like Melchizedek?

    1. (John 1:49, Rev. 19:16) Jesus is...

    2. (4:14) Jesus is...

e. What did Abraham do when he met Melchizedek? (7:2 and 4)

f. What did this prove about Melchizedek? (7:7)

g. What about Jesus in this respect? (See John 8:53 and 58)

7a. What does the fact that God appointed another Head Priest like Melchizedek show about the Levitical priests? (7:11)

b. What is it that qualified Jesus as the perfect Head Priest? (vs 16)

   1. Not His...

   2. but the fact that He possessed...

8. What sort of a guarantee did God give us when He appointed Jesus with an oath? (7:22)

9. What advantages do we have because Jesus is an eternal, ever-living Head Priest? (vs 25)

   1. (RSV, Beck)

   2.

10a. How does the fact that Jesus is without sin set Him apart from all the head priests of the Old Covenant? (vs 27a)

  b. What therefore was the difference between the sacrifice He offered and theirs? (vs 27b)

11. What does all this (questions 8-10) mean so far as Jesus is concerned? (vs 28, last phrase)

12a. Read chapter 8. What about the sanctuary in which Jesus carries on His work? (vs 2)

  b. What about the sanctuary in which the Levitical priests worked? (vs 5)

  c. What about the work Jesus is doing? (vs 6a)

  d. Why is the new covenant better than the old one? (vs 6c)

13a. What was the matter with the Old Covenant? (vs 9c)

  b. What then did he say was happening to the Old Covenant? (vs 13b)

     1.   2.

14a. Read 9:1-10. What were the names of the two rooms in the old tabernacle? (vss 2-3)

     1.   2.

  b. Where did the priests carry on their work? (vs 6)

c. Who was the only one allowed in the Most Holy Place? (vs 7a)

d. How often was he allowed to enter? (vs 7a)

e. What was this day called? (Lev. 23:27)

f. What was God teaching the people of Israel by allowing the Head Priest to enter only once a year? (vs 8, RSV)

g. What then was the significance of the tearing apart of the curtain in the Temple on the day Jesus died? (Matt. 27:51)

15a. Read 9:11-18. Why was the sacrifice Jesus offered to God much better than the sacrifices offered under the Old Covenant? (vs 12)

    1. It was not...

    2. but...

b. What did Jesus' sacrifice accomplish for us? (vs 12b)

c. What does this do for us? (vs 14b)

16a. What is Jesus called in vs 15a?

b. What are we going to receive under this new covenant? (vs 15b)

17a. What must happen before a will becomes effective? (vs 17)

b. Read 9:19-28. Who died to put the Old Covenant at Sinai into effect? (vs 19)

c. What principle is thus established? (vs 22b)

18. How does the writer sum up this whole section in vs 26b?

19a. What two things must happen to every human being? (vs 27)

    1.

    2.

b. How did or will Jesus share in these same two experiences? (vs 28)

    1.

    2.

20a. Read 10:1-18. What therefore is the Law? (vs 1, see Col. 2:17)

   b. What does this mean in a practical way? (vs 1b)

   c. What did the sacrifices of the Old Covenant do for the people? (vs 3)

   d. Why? (vs 4)

21. What did Jesus' one sacrifice do for the world of men? (vss 10, 14)

22a. Read 10:19-39. What has Jesus' sacrifice made of us? (Is. 61:6, Rev. 1:6, I Peter 2:9, second phrase)

   b. What has Jesus' death done for us? (vs 20)

   c. What are we to do, therefore? (vs 19)

   d. What is this Most Holy Place? (vs 22a)

      The place where...

23. Why is it possible for us to come into God's presence now? (vs 22b)

24a. What however will destroy our holiness and cause us to forfeit our salvation? (vs 26)

   b. What is there left for us if this happens? (vs 27)

   c. What solemn reminder does the writer give us in this respect? (vs 31)

25a. What had happened to the Christians to whom this letter was addressed? (vss 32b-33a)

   b. How had they acted at the time? (vs 34b)

   c. Why? (vs 34c)

26. What did the writer urge them to do now?

      1. (vs 35)

      2. (vs 36)

27a. Read chapter 11. How does the writer define faith? (vs 1, NIV, Beck)

   b. What is one example of such faith? (vs 3)

28a. Read 12:1-11. Since all these heroes of faith (chapter 11) are watching us, what must we do? (vs 1)

   1.

   2.

   3.

   b. And what must we do as we run? (vs 2a)

29a. How does He serve as our example? (vs 2b, KJ)

   1.

   2.

   b. Why should we use Him as our example? (vs 3)

30a. What about their former persecutions and sufferings? (vs 4)

   b. How must we all look upon persecution and sufferings? (vss 5b-6)

   c. Why does God discipline us? (vs 10b)

31a. Read 12:12-29. What instructions does the writer give in vs 14a?

   b. What warning does he give in 14b? (compare Rev. 21:27a)

32a. Read chapter 13. Of what did the writer remind his readers in vs 14?

   1.

   2.

   b. What sort of a sacrifice should we bring to God?

   1. (vs 15b)

   2. (vs 16a)

   3. (vs 16a)

33a. What news did he send in vs 23a?

   b. What were the writer's plans? (vs 23b)

LESSON 31 - JOHN'S THREE LETTERS
90-94 A.D.

<u>I John</u> (John probably left Jerusalem just before the city was destroyed by the Romans in 70 A.D., and went to Ephesus, where he lived to be a very old man. He probably wrote this letter between 90 and 94 A.D. Like Hebrews, it has no greetings or signature, but it was probably written to the same churches around Ephesus that Paul wrote to earlier in "Ephesians", since the error John wrote against here was a form of Gnosticism, which denied that Jesus was the Son of God or that He took on a true human body and lived and died as a true man).

1a. Read 1:1-4. What is this letter about? (vs 1, last phrase)

b. What does the writer say about this Word? (vs 1a, see John 1:1)

c. What do we learn when we compare vs 1a with the first 4 verses of the Gospel of John?

d. What other information does John give about the Word in vs 1b?

   1.

   2.

   3.

2a. Read 1:5-10. Where did this message come from? (vs 5a, compare question 1)

b. What was the first great truth about God? (vs 5b)

c. What does this mean to us in a practical way? (vs 6)

d. What assurance do we have if we're living in the light? (vs 7)

   1.

   2.

3a. What was one of the errors of the Gnostics? (vss 8a, 10a, NIV)

b. What does John say about this?

   1. (vs 8b)

   2. (vs 10b)

4a. What must we do when we sin? (vs 9a)

b. What does God then do for us? (vs 9b)

    1.

    2.

5a. Read 2:1-6. What was one reason John wrote this letter? (vs 1a)

b. What comfort do we Christians have when we do sin? (vs 1b, see Heb. 7:25b)

c. What did Jesus do for us? (vs 2a, NIV, Beck)

d. For whom did Jesus make His sacrifice? (vs 2b)

    1. Not...   2. but...

6a. What about the one who says, "I know Him," but doesn't keep His commandments? (vs 4)

b. What does John say about the person who does what Jesus tells him? (vs 5, NIV)

c. What rule must we follow if we say we are "in Jesus"? (vs 6, Beck)

7a. What was the "new commandment" Jesus gave in vs 10a? (See John 13:34)

b. What does John say about the professing Christian who hates his brother? (vs 9)

c. What about the person who loves his brother? (vs 10a)

8a. Read 2:15-17. What is the second commandment the Lord gave us? (vs 15a)

b. What does John say about the person who loves the world? (vs 15b)

c. Why is this? (vs 16b)

d. What are some of these "things" of the world? (vs 16a)

    1.

    2.

    3.

e. What is going to happen to the world? (vs 17a, see II Pet. 3:10)

f. What about the person who does what God wants? (vs 17b)

9a. Read 2:18-28. What period of time are we living in now? (vs 18a)

b. To what future event did John point in vs 18b? (See II Thess. 2:3-4 and 8)

   c. What did John say had already happened there in Asia? (vs 18c)

   d. Where did he say these antichrists had come from? (vs 19a)

10a. How could they recognize one of these false teachers? (vs 22b)

   b. What basic truth is set forth in vs 23? (Compare John 10:30)

      1. (vs 23a)

      2. (vs 23b)

11a. How can we protect ourselves from all false teachers? (vs 24a)

   b. What will happen if we keep all these things in our hearts? (vs 24b)

   c. What do we call living with the Father and the Son? (vs 25, see John 5:24)

12a. What was another reason John wrote this letter? (vs 26)

   b. What was the "anointing" they had received from God? (vs 27a, see 3:24c)

   c. What did the fact that the Spirit was in their hearts mean in a practical way? (vs 27b)

   d. Why? (vs 27c, compare John 14:26)

13. Why is it so important that we keep on living in Jesus? (vs 28)

14a. Read 2:29-3:3. What is one thing we know about God? (vs 29a)

   b. And because of this, what else do we know? (vs 29b)

15a. What amazing thing has God done for us in His love? (3:1a)

   b. And why doesn't the world like (know) us? (vs 1b)

16a. What does John say about our future? (vs 2b)

   b. What is one thing we know will happen to us when Jesus returns? (vs 2c)

   c. What does every sincere Christian do therefore? (vs 3)

17a. Read 3:4-24. What is John's definition of sin? (vs 4b)

b. What did Jesus come to do? (vs 5a)

18a. What is one important thing about the person who lives in Jesus? (vs 6a)

  b. What about the person who does keep on sinning? (vs 6b)

19a. What does God say about the child of God who does what is right? (vs 7a)

  b. What about the person who keeps on sinning? (vs 8a)

20. What is one main reason Jesus came into the world? (vs 8c, compare Gen. 3:15)

21. What comfort does the fact that we love our brothers give us? (vs 14a)

22. What does John say about the person who hates his brother? (vs 15)

23a. How do we know what love is? (vs 16a)

  b. What should we do, then, as God's children? (vs 16b)

  c. How does John sum up this discussion of Christian love? (vs 18, compare James 2:14-17)

24a. Read 4:1-6. What warning did John give his readers? (vs 1a)

  b. What is one good test of a true prophet? (vs 2)

25a. What comforting thought did John give his readers in vs 4a?

  b. Why? (vs 4b, compare John 16:33b)

26. How can we recognize the Spirit of truth and the spirit of error? (vs 6a)

    1.

    2.

27a. Read 4:7-21. Where does Christian love come from? (vs 7a)

  b. What is the second great truth about God? (vs 8b)

  c. How did God show His love for us? (vs 9, see John 3:16)

  d. What then is the real picture of love? (vs 10)

    1. Not that...

       2. but that...

28a. What has happened to us if we love each other? (vs 12, RSV)

    1.

    2.

  b. When does this indwelling of God in us begin? (vs 15, RSV, Beck)

  c. What effect will this have on us on Judgment Day? (vs 17a)

29. Why do we love God? (vs 19)

30. Read 5:1-5. How do we show our love for God? (vss 2-3a)

31. What comforting thought does John give us in vs 4a? (RSV, Beck)

32a. Read 5:6-20, and remember that the Gnostics denied the fact that Jesus was born as a God-man and died as a God-man. They thought that He was just a man, and that the Spirit came upon Him at His baptism (by water), but left Him again before He died (by blood).

What fact, therefore, does John emphasize in vs 6a?

  b. How does John summarize God's message in vs 11?

  c. What does this mean so far as we are concerned? (vs 12)

    1.

    2.

33. What was John's main purpose in writing this letter? (vs 13, compare also 2:1 and 2:26)

34. What is the one sin which will never be forgiven? (vs 16b, see also Mark 3:28-29)

35. What was John's last emphatic thought?

    1. (20a)

    2. (20c)

II John (This letter was probably written about the same time as
I John. It was addressed to some individual church in Asia
Minor, and was also written to warn against false teachers,
no doubt Gnostics).

36a. Read the whole letter. To whom was it addressed? (vs 1,
remember that the word for church is feminine)

b. What commandment does John repeat at the beginning? (vs 5)

c. What does this mean in a practical way? (vs 6)

37a. What warning did he send in vs 7a?

b. What was his next warning? (vs 8a)

c. What in particular does he warn against in vs 9a?

38. What orders does he give them in vs 10?

III John (This letter was written to a prominent member of one of
the churches in Asia who had been an ardent supporter of the
Lord's work there, opening his home to all the visiting preachers sent out by John the apostle. He was having rouble,
however, with another man who was trying to take control of
the church there. The letter was probably written about the
same time as the other two).

39a. Read the whole letter. To whom was it addressed? (vs 1)

b. What good news had John received which made him happy? (vs 4)

c. What had Gaius been doing for the travelling preachers?
(vss 5 & 8)

40a. What problem was there? (vs 9, RSV, Beck)

b. What else was Diotrephes doing?

1. (vs 10b)

2. (vs 10c)

3. (vs 10d)

41a. What did John ask Gaius to do? (vs 11a)

b. What were John's plans? (vs 14)

LESSON 32 - SUMMARY

The first page of Acts makes it clear that the author was _____, whose first book told of what Jesus ____ and _____, and ended with His _____ into _____, which is exactly where Acts begins. The first scene opens with Jesus and His followers gathered on the Mt. of _____, speaking of the Kingdom of Heaven; and Jesus told them that soon they would be _____ with the _____ _____. Then they would be filled with _____ and would become His _____ in _____, _____ and _____, and to the _____ ends of the _____. Then He began to _____ into _____, and soon He was _____. Next, two _____ told them that Jesus would _____ _____ again in the _____ _____ He had just left.

Ten days later, on _____, all of Jesus' disciples were _____ with the _____ _____, and began to _____ in other _____. When a crowd gathered because of the noise, _____ delivered a sermon to them, stressing Jesus' _____ and _____, and _____ people were brought to _____ in Jesus. And in the days that followed _____ kept on _____ more people to their group every day.

A short while later _____ worked a remarkable _____ through _____ and _____, when they _____ a _____ man in the Temple-yard. After this Peter told the crowd that they had _____ their _____ whom God had sent them, and that they must _____ of their ____. When the Jewish authorities saw what was happening, they _____ Peter and John, and the next day, when they began to question them, Peter told them that Jesus is the _____ _____ who can _____ us. The authorities then

177

threatened them and let them go.

At this time all the believers were of _____ mind and heart. Some of them even sold their _____ and _____ and gave the _____ to the _____ to _____ to the _____. And every day the apostles kept on telling the people about Jesus' _____-_____, and Jesus kept on working _____ through the _____, so that many _____ people were _____. This made the priests and Sadducees so angry that they _____ Peter and John again and put them in _____; and the next day they told Peter and John that they must stop _____ the people about _____, but Peter told them, "One must _____ ____ rather than men."

Soon the group of Christians, or _____, as they called themselves, became so large that the apostles were spending nearly all their time passing out _____ and _____ to the poor; and so they elected _____ other men to serve as their _____. These men were called _____, and one of them, named _____, preached about _____ so powerfully that the Jews _____ him. The man in charge of the lynching was a young Pharisee named _____, who now stirred up the Jews so that a great _____ broke out against the Church in _____, which caused the believers to _____ all over _____ and _____. But instead of destroying the Church, as the Jews hoped to do, this caused the good _____ to _____ over a wider area. The leader of the work in Samaria was _____, another of the deacons, and many people believed what he told them when they saw the _____ the Lord was doing through him.

After a while _____, the leader of the persecution, decided to go to _____ to _____ all the Christians there and bring them back to _____. But just before he got to the city the _____ appeared to him in a great blaze of _____ and _____ to him, asking him why he was _____ Him. As a result _____ was also brought to _____ in _____, and was _____; and right away he began to _____ in the synagogues that Jesus is _____ ____. When he got back to Jerusalem, he did the same thing, and some of the Jews tried to _____ him; and so His new friends sent him home to _____. This ended the _____.

During the next few years the apostles _____ all around _____ the work and _____ the people what Jesus had told them, but the book of Acts tells us only about the activities of _____ , who travelled around _____ and _____. When he was in Joppa the Lord worked a remarkable _____ when Peter _____ a lady who had _____ back to _____. As a result _____ people came to _____ in _____.

While Peter was in Joppa an _____ appeared to a Roman army captain named _____ who lived in Caesarea, and told him to _____ for _____. And the next day Peter saw a _____ in which he saw a big _____ coming down from _____, full of _____ kinds of _____, reptiles and _____. God was using this to teach Peter that there are no longer any distinctions between _____ and _____ people, and that the Church is to be made up of people of all _____ who _____ in Him, the _____ God, and do what is _____. The next day Peter told _____ and his friends about _____, and His _____ and _____. And while Peter was speaking the _____ _____ came down on _____ there. The Jewish believers were _____ when they saw that God had poured out His _____

_____ on people who weren't _____; but when Peter saw this, he gave orders that they should all be _____. When Peter got back to Jerusalem the Jewish believers _____ him because he had gone into the _____ of a _____ and _____ with him; but when Peter _____ what had happened, they realized that God also brings _____ to _____ so that they too can have _____ _____.

Some of the believers who left Jerusalem during the persecution went into the neighboring lands of Phoenicia, Syria and Cyprus; and the ones who went to Antioch did something new - they began to bring the message to people who _____ _____, or even proselytes, like Cornelius; and it was there in Antioch that the believers were first called _____.

It was probably about 43 A.D. that the first government persecution of the Church began under _____ Agrippa I. One of the first to be killed was the apostle _____. Agrippa also imprisoned _____, but the Lord delivered him miraculously, and after _____ sudden death, the persecution ended.

About this same time _____, the Lord's _____, who was now the _____ of the Church in Jerusalem, wrote a letter to the _____ Christians who had been scattered about in all the _____ by the first _____. Many of them were poor, and therefore they were having many _____, but he told them to look on their troubles as something _____, because troubles _____ our _____ and make us _____ Christians. He also warned them that most of our temptations to sin come from our own _____ _____, and told them that the secret of a holier Christian life is to _____ to God's _____ and _____ it.

He also wrote that if one keeps the _____ ____ of Moses, and then sins in just _____ _____, he has broken the _____ ____, and is subject to _____ _____, and that if one knows what is right and doesn't do it, this is a ____ of _____. And he said that our faith must be _____ and produce all kinds of _____ _____ to be a _____ faith.

In 47 the Holy Spirit moved the church in Antioch to send out _____ and _____ as their first foreign missionaries. Their first stop was the island of _____, where Paul found his first audience in the Jewish _____. His next stop was Antioch in Pisidia, where Paul followed the same procedure. Here Luke sums up Paul's message in three points - 1) forgiveness of sins comes through _____; 2) we are justified or declared to be perfect in God's sight by _____, 3) and not through the _____. After many proselytes and gentiles were brought to faith, the _____ stirred up _____ for Paul, a pattern which repeated itself everywhere he went. It was there also that Paul called himself a _____ for the _____, and said that his work was to bring _____ to the _____ of the earth. Paul and Barnabas then went into some of the cities in Galatia, where Paul reminded his hearers that to get into God's Kingdom we must go through a lot of _____ and _____. Then they retraced their steps and went home to Antioch and made their report.

About this time some Jews from Jerusalem came down to Antioch and told the gentile believers that they must be _____ to be saved; and this stirred up such an argument that the group sent _____ and _____ to Jerusalem to meet with the Church there about this matter. When all the apostles and elders had gathered, Peter told them about his experiences with _____ and said that our hearts can be made clean from sin only by _____; and the Church finally agreed that circumcision is not _____, since everyone is saved by _____; and they sent a letter back to Antioch telling them of this decision.

Paul's first letter was written in 50 to his new churches in _____ because the same kind of Jews who had recently been in Antioch had also gone there, telling the gentiles that they must be _____ and _____ the _____ Law to be saved. Paul told them about the meeting in Jerusalem, that Titus, who was a gentile, had not been required to be _____, and said that the Church had never _____ these ideas. He said that the true children of Abraham are those who _____ in _____, as Abraham did, and that those who depend on the Law for salvation are under a _____. But _____, he said, has removed this _____ from us. Thus Paul's main point in this letter is that "those who are righteous by _____ have _____ _____," since the Law had been given after the Promise, and was given to be the Jews' _____ until _____ came. Thus Jesus has set us _____ from the Law, but we must not use this _____ as an _____ to _____.

Soon after sending this letter Paul started out on his second missionary _____. He took _____ along, and picked up _____ in Lystra. When they got to Troas, _____ joined the group, and they crossed over into Europe for the first time, going to Philippi. While they were in jail there, the jailer asked them how he could be saved, and Paul replied, "_____ in the _____ _____ _____, and you'll be saved;" and when Paul spoke in the synagogue in Thessalonica, his two main points were that 1) as the Messiah Jesus had to _____ and 2)then _____ again from the _____.

When Paul arrived in Berea, the Jews there set us a good example as true believers. They _____ the Scriptures _____ _____ to see if what Paul told them was _____. But when the Jews from Thessalonica found out Paul was in Berea, they caused so much trouble that Paul had to leave; and he visited Athens briefly and went on to Corinth. As soon as he arrived, he wrote a letter to the Christians in Thessalonica because he had heard that they were worried about the believers who had _____, thinking that they would not be able to get into the Kingdom of _____. Paul praised them because they had received his message as _____ _____, and told them that God wants all believers to be _____. Then he assured them that Christ would _____ all the believers back with Him when He _____, because they will all _____ from the _____ as Jesus descends. He also reminded them that the Day of Jesus' return will come _____, like a _____ in the _____.

A short while later Paul learned that the believers in Thessalonica were alarmed because they had heard that the Day of the Lord had _____ _____, so he wrote them another letter in which he told them that eternal death is being _____ _____ from God's presence in the Kingdom of Glory, and assured them that the Day of the Lord cannot come until the great _____ against _____ takes place and the _____ _____ is unmasked, who is also called the _____. He said that this man will set himself up in _____ _____ and claim to be _____; and when he is unmasked, he will be _____. And finally Paul told them that we Christians must always remember that God _____ us to be His _____ _____ in _____. And this means that we have to be made

_____; and that this is the work of the _____ _____, which He begins when He brings us to _____. And all this gives us _____ comfort and a wonderful _____.

In 53 Paul left Antioch for his third missionary trip. Again he visited the churches in Galatia and then went to _____, the capital city of Asia. Not long after he arrived, he received word that the Christians in Corinth were also having troubles, and so he sent them a letter - First _____. He assured them that in all our troubles Christ will _____ us _____ to the end, and focussed their attention on the cross, telling them that it is _____ to those who are perishing, but for us it is the _____ of _____. In fact, Paul summed up his message by saying, "we preach nothing except _____ _____, and Him _____;" and said that Jesus is the only _____ for the Church, which he called God's _____. He warned them that the _____ will never inherit God's Kingdom, and reminded them that we can get into the Kingdom because we have been _____ and _____ by the _____ _____. One of their problems was the Lord's Supper, and Paul told them that when we drink the _____ we are _____ Christ's _____, and when we eat the _____, we are _____ His _____. Then he warned them that anyone who eats and drinks in an _____ manner is _____ against Christ, and that whoever eats and drinks without _____ Christ's body is _____ by his eating and drinking. Another problem concerned the _____ of the Spirit, and so Paul reminded them that the Spirit passes them out so that each Christian can do something _____ in the Kingdom. He said that the greatest of all gifts is Christian _____, and that we must all use our gifts to _____ others. There were also some Christians in Corinth who felt that there could be no such thing as a _____, and Paul said that the answer to this was that _____ was _____. He also assured them that _____ is going to be _____ again.

Not long after he wrote this letter Paul learned that some new preachers arrived in Corinth who were _____ the minds of the Christians against Paul, and so Paul wrote a _____ letter in which he told them that his credentials as a true apostle were all the things he had _____ for Christ, and reminded them that when we are _____ we are _____.

Then, after the Christians in Corinth had gotten rid of the men who were causing the trouble, and had solved their problems Paul wrote them a _____ letter, in which he reminded them that we are all being _____ into the likeness of _____ by _____ at Him in all His _____ as we see Him in His Word, and that at the present time we are _____ from our Lord, so that we all feel that we would rather _____ this world and be at _____ with the _____. But while we're here our one great aim is to _____ Christ our Lord, for it is our _____ for Him which _____ our lives and all our actions. He also reminded them that every Christian is a new _____, and that in Christ God has reconciled the _____ _____ to Himself. He then warned them that they must not _____ with unbelievers. And when he wrote about the collection for the poor, Paul said that the first principle in Christian giving is to give _____ to the Lord, and that the only true motive for giving is Christ's _____ for us.

When Paul left Ephesus, he travelled around Macedonia and Greece picking up the money for the poor in Jerusalem, and when he came back to Corinth in 57, he wrote a letter to the Christians in Rome to tell them that he was going to stop there on his trip to Spain. He also wanted to give them a short summary of the Christian faith, and he began by reminding them that the Gospel is the _____ of _____ that brings _____ to every one who _____ it, because it brings one Christ's _____, which makes one _____ in God's sight. The Law, however, can never make anyone _____ in God's sight because no one can _____ the Law. God gave the Law to _____ us our _____. He then told them that sin came into the world through _____ and _____ at the _____, and that as a result of that one sin ____ ____ were made _____. But through the work of _____ all men have been made _____ or perfect. Therefore we Christians cannot go on living in _____, because we have _____ ·to _____ when we were _____, so that we can live a ____ life, and the _____ _____ controls our life now. Our problem, however, is that we all still have our old _____ flesh, which is so corrupt that there isn't ____ _____ thing in it, and this explains why we keep on doing things we _____ want to do, and _____ to do the _____ things we _____ to do. He also told them that our present troubles can't even be _____ with the glory God is going to give us, and that the Spirit helps us in our troubles by _____ for us. And we know that _____ works for our _____, because God decided in _____ that we should all be like _____, and He is the one who has _____ us to faith. Who, then, can accuse us of any ____ when God has already declared us to be _____? And who can _____ us when Jesus, who _____ for us is going to be our _____? Thus we can be absolutely confident that _____ can _____ us from God's love.

On his way back to Jerusalem Paul stopped at Troas for a service on _____, and when a young man fell out of the window and died, Paul _____ him back to _____. When he got back to Jerusalem, the Jews attacked him, and the Roman Governor arrested Paul as a safety measure; but he was kept in prison for ____ _____, from 57 to 59. Finally Paul used his right as a Roman citizen and appealed his case to the Roman _____.

On his way to Rome Paul's ship was caught in a _____; but they finally landed safely at the island of _____, where Paul _____ a lot of people. When he arrived in Rome, in 59, he was allowed to live in his own _____ _____, and he lived there for ____ years, waiting for his trial, during which time he kept on spreading the _____ about God's _____ and _____ the Christians there what the Scriptures say about _____.

During Paul's imprisonment a slave named _____ ran away from his master and made his way to Rome. Since his master _____ was a friend of Paul's the slave came to Paul, and after Paul brought him to _____, he sent him back to his master with a letter, asking the master to _____ his slave _____ again as a _____ Christian and _____ him. At the same time Paul sent another letter to the congregation in Colossae because some false teachers called _____ had come to town and were misleading the people. Since these people claimed to have special _____, Paul wrote that the only kind of knowledge he wanted them to have was that which _____ from ____; and the treasures of wisdom and knowledge are to be found in _____. Therefore we Christians must keep our eyes fixed on the things in _____, where _____ is.

Then along with these two letters Paul sent a third letter to all the churches in Asia. Because it was to be read first in Ephesus, it is called _____, and like Colossians, it was written to warn against the _____. Here also Paul focussed their attention on _____, who has won our _____, or the _____ of sins, and who rules over _____ in _____ and on _____ in the interest of His _____. Paul also reminded them that before we were brought to faith, we were all in the _____, but now we are living in the _____.

Next Paul wrote to his friends in Philippi to encourage them by telling them that He who has begun the good work in us will _____ on _____ to make it _____ until the day of _____ _____. And he told them that as he looked forward to his trial, he felt that to live is _____, and to die is _____, and that he didn't want a righteousness of ____ ____, but the righteousness that comes from ____ through _____ in _____. Then he told them that when Christ returns, He is going to _____ our lowly _____ so that they will be _____ His _____ body.

At Paul's trial in 62 he was found not _____ and released; and at once he started travelling again, going to Crete, Ephesus and Philippi. From Philippi he wrote a letter to Timothy, whom he had left in Ephesus to oversee the work there. Timothy was to remind the believers that Jesus came into the world to _____ _____, and that God wants ____ ____ to be saved and come to the _____ of the _____. He was also to remind them that we brought _____ into the world, and we can _____ _____ out, and that if we have _____ and _____, we must be _____, for those who want to be rich fall into _____ and a trap, because the _____ of money is a _____ of ____ _____ of _____. Therefore we Christians must use our money to do _____ things for _____.

Then Paul wrote a short letter to Titus, whom he had left in Crete to oversee the work there, telling him to remind the Christians that our great blessed hope is Jesus' final _____ in glory, and that the special means God uses to save us is _____, by which we are _____ _____ and filled with _____ _____ by the _____.

Shortly after Paul left Rome, Peter arrived there, and in 63 or 64 he wrote a letter to the Christians living in Asia Minor (modern Turkey), who were being persecuted because of their faith. Peter reminded them that the source of our Christian hope is Christ's _____ from the _____, which will bring us an inheritance that can never be _____; and that God's purpose in allowing sufferings and troubles to come to us is to _____ our faith and prove that it is _____; and that we Christians are like people living in a _____ land, and that we are now God's _____ people. In his second letter Peter said that God's _____ is even more dependable than his own eyewitness testimony, and that the Scriptures were written by the _____ _____, who took control of the _____ so that they wrote what God _____ them to write. He also told them that on the last Day the world will be destroyed by _____, and the heavens will _____ with a roar, and that then God will create a _____ heavens and a _____ _____.

About 65 or 66 Paul was arrested again and Peter also, during Nero's great persecution of the Church, and before his trial and death Paul wrote one last letter to Timothy in Ephesus, telling him that all _____ will have their share of _____, especially during the last days before the end, which will be a _____ time to live, for in those days people will love

_____ and _____ and _____ more than ____. Then he urged Timothy to hold fast to the Scriptures, which are _____ by ____. Paul and Peter were killed soon after this.

After the persecution Apollos probably wrote the letter to the Hebrews, Jewish Christians who were still being persecuted by other Jews. He reminded them that God made His final full revelation of Himself through His ____, and that Jesus is far better than the _____, far better than _____, through whom God made the first covenant, and far better than the Old Testament _____ _____, because He is God's ____, and is _____ and _____. Thus He is _____ able to _____ us, and is _____ living to _____ for us, and He offered a far _____ sacrifice, because it was His ____ blood, which has purchased an _____ inheritance for us and has made ____ men holy and perfectly _____ from ____.

Before the fall of Jerusalem in 70, John moved from Jerusalem to Ephesus, where he lived to be a very old man. While he was there he wrote _____ letters to the same congregations around Ephesus to which Paul had written earlier. He reminded the believers that Jesus' blood makes us _____ from every ____, and that Jesus died not only for us Christians, but for the _____ _____, and that we Christians must love _____ _____, but not the _____. He also said that we are living in the last _____ before Jesus' _____, and that _____ Antichrists have come into the world. He also reminded us that living with the Father and the Son is _____ _____, and that when Jesus returns, we are going to be just _____ Him, and that Jesus came into the world to _____ everything the _____ has done. And he said that he wrote his letter so that we who _____ in _____ will have _____ ____.